Navigating Cybersecurity and Ethical Hacking

**The Art of Ethical Hacking:
Exploring Cybersecurity from Within**

Lily Grayson

Table of Contents

INTRODUCTION

The idea of security has completely changed in our digital world, as technology permeates every aspect of our lives. New avenues for invention and communication have been made possible by the internet's extensive interconnection, smartphones' rapid growth, computers, and Internet of Things devices. But there is an extraordinary amount of risk that has been brought to us by the digital revolution.

Cyber threats have become commonplace, ranging from advanced malware and nation-state cyber-espionage to data breaches and identity theft. The world needs heroes to confront these obstacles; it requires protectors of the digital space with the expertise, ethical framework, and abilities to take on cyber adversaries. Ethical hackers are these heroes.

Welcome to "Navigating Cybersecurity and Ethical Hacking: The Art of Ethical Hacking - Exploring Cybersecurity from Within." Your ticket to the fascinating and dynamic world of ethical hacking and cybersecurity is this book. You will go from learning the basics of cybersecurity to becoming an expert in the field of ethical hacking on this adventure.

We shall investigate the various facets of hackers, solve the mysteries surrounding hacking, and differentiate between ethical and malicious hacking on the pages that follow. We will delve into the realm of cyberthreats and vulnerabilities, giving you the skills necessary to recognize and successfully reduce risks.

As we go along, we'll reveal the process that ethical hackers use and provide you real tasks and examples to make sure you understand the concepts in theory as well as acquire practical abilities. We will examine penetration testing in detail and highlight its significance for protecting digital systems.

However, this book covers defense in addition to hacking. We'll talk about security policies, cybersecurity best practices, and the importance of security awareness training in building a strong defense against online threats.

As you go, you'll come across actual case studies that demonstrate how effective ethical hacking can be in defending individuals as well as businesses. We'll analyze each of these situations, taking away important moral lessons and insights.

We've devoted a chapter to career options in the exciting topic of ethical hacking for individuals who are thinking about making a profession out of it. We'll walk you through the skills and expertise needed to be successful as an ethical hacker and offer advice on how to create a fulfilling profession.

Finally, we will look to the future of cybersecurity. We'll look at new technology, impending risks, and the precautions we need to take to keep our distance from cybercriminals.

It's critical to keep in mind the importance of ethical hacking in our increasingly connected society as we set out on our journey. In order to protect our digital infrastructure, protect our privacy, and maintain the fundamentals of cybersecurity, ethical hackers are essential.

So, this book is your guide if you're interested in hacking and digital protection, an enthusiast for cybersecurity, or just want to learn more about it. Come along as we delve into the practice of ethical hacking and examine the broad field of cybersecurity from the inside out. In unison, we shall ascend to the role of digital stewards, prepared to meet the obstacles that lie ahead in the digital era.

CHAPTER I

Understanding Cybersecurity

Defining cybersecurity

Within the swiftly changing digital age environment, cybersecurity stands as the bastion protecting our interconnected world from an ever-growing array of threats. Defining cybersecurity requires us to delve deep into the realm of technology, data, and the digital infrastructures upon which our modern society relies. Cybersecurity encompasses the strategies, practices, and technologies that safeguard our digital systems, networks, and sensitive information from illegal access, malicious attacks, and data breaches.

One fundamental aspect of defining cybersecurity is recognizing that it is not a static concept but a dynamic and adaptive discipline. In essence, cybersecurity is a continuous process, a journey rather than a destination. It involves the constant assessment of vulnerabilities, the implementation of protective measures, and the adaptation to emerging threats. It's a proactive and ongoing effort to keep the privacy, integrity, and availability of data and systems.

Confidentiality, the first pillar of cybersecurity, revolves around ensuring that sensitive information stays accessible only to those who have the proper authorization. It involves encryption, access controls, and secure communication channels. Protecting confidentiality means that personal data, financial records, trade secrets, and classified information remain shielded from prying eyes and potential adversaries.

Integrity is the second crucial element of cybersecurity. It pertains to the accuracy and trustworthiness of data and systems. Ensuring data integrity means that information remains unaltered and reliable. Any unauthorized modification or tampering with data can have severe consequences, from misinformation to system failures. Thus, cybersecurity focuses on measures to detect and prevent unauthorized changes, such as checksums and digital signatures.

Availability forms the third cornerstone of cybersecurity.

It signifies the need for data and systems to be accessible when needed. Availability concerns the prevention of downtime, disruptions, and denial-of-service attacks. Maintaining the availability of critical systems is vital for businesses, governments, as well as individuals who rely on technology for their daily operations.

As we explore the dimensions of cybersecurity, it's essential to recognize the diverse range of threats it must combat. Cyber threats come in various forms, from the relatively mundane, such as viruses and phishing scams, to the highly sophisticated, including advanced persistent threats (APTs) and zero-day exploits. Each threat poses unique challenges, requiring cybersecurity professionals to employ a multifaceted approach to defense.

Cybersecurity also extends beyond individual organizations and individuals. It encompasses the broader cybersecurity ecosystem, involving governments, businesses, law enforcement agencies, and international collaborations. Cybersecurity regulations and standards are continually evolving, reflecting the increasing importance of this field. Adherence to these regulations is both legally mandated and an essential component of risk management.

One of the defining characteristics of cybersecurity is its interdisciplinary nature. It draws from various domains, including computer science, information technology, cryptography, risk management, and even psychology. Understanding human behavior and social engineering techniques is essential to mitigate threats like phishing attacks, where attackers exploit human vulnerabilities rather than technical flaws.

Moreover, the ethical dimension of cybersecurity should not be overlooked. The field is not solely about defending against threats but also about upholding principles of privacy, transparency, and accountability. Ethical considerations are particularly relevant in the context of ethical hacking or penetration testing, where professionals simulate cyberattacks to uncover vulnerabilities and strengthen defenses.

Defining cybersecurity is, therefore, a complex task that involves understanding its multifaceted nature, its goals of ensuring confidentiality, integrity, and availability, and its continual adaptation to the evolving threat landscape. In essence, cybersecurity is the vigilant guardian of our digital age, working tirelessly to protect our digital lives, our data, and the critical systems that underpin our modern world. It is not a choice but an imperative—a constant and collective effort to safeguard the foundations of our interconnected society from those who would seek to exploit its vulnerabilities.

Historical context and evolution of cybersecurity

The history of cybersecurity is an enthralling journey through the annals of technology and human innovation. It is a tale of the ever-escalating battle between those who create digital systems and those who seek to exploit their vulnerabilities. To understand the present and future of cybersecurity, one must delve into its historical context and evolution, tracing the origins of cyber threats and the measures taken to defend against them.

The roots of cybersecurity can be traced back to the early days of computing, a time when computers were room-sized machines, and networks were in their infancy. In these nascent years, the primary concern was not so much protecting information from malicious actors but rather ensuring the integrity and reliability of data and machines themselves. Early computer systems were vulnerable to hardware failures, and engineers focused on building redundancy and fault tolerance into these systems to mitigate such risks. Security, as we know it today, was not a central concern.

However, as computing technology advanced and computer systems became more interconnected, vulnerabilities began to emerge. In the 1960s and 1970s, the first instances of computer viruses and malware appeared. These were relatively simple compared to today's threats but marked the beginning of a new era. The "Creeper" program, which showed the text "I'm the creeper, catch me if you can!" on affected machines, was among the first known examples of malware. It was, in essence, a benign experiment, but it highlighted the potential for unauthorized code execution on computer systems.

The 1980s saw a significant uptick in cyber incidents. The advent of personal computers and the proliferation of early networking technologies like ARPANET laid the groundwork for more extensive cyberattacks. In 1986, the first computer worm, known as the "Morris Worm," infected thousands of computers, causing considerable disruption. This incident prompted increased attention to computer security, leading to the formation of the first Computer Emergency Response Team (or CERT) at Carnegie Mellon University.

As the 1990s dawned, the internet became a global phenomenon, connecting people and systems across the world. The rapid growth of online communication and ecommerce brought with it new opportunities for cybercriminals. The decade witnessed the rise of hacking as a subculture, with notable incidents like the defacement of websites and the proliferation of hacking tools. It was during this period that the term "cybersecurity" began to gain traction.

The late 1990s and early 2000s witnessed a dramatic escalation in cyber threats. High-profile incidents, such as the "ILOVEYOU" virus and the "Code Red" worm, garnered global attention. The consequences of these attacks were not merely technical but had real-world economic and social impacts. Governments and businesses alike recognized the need to take cybersecurity seriously.

In response to the developing cyber threat landscape, governments and international organizations began to develop cybersecurity policies and regulations. The U.S. government, for instance, established the National Infrastructure Protection Center (NIPC) in 1998 and later the Department of Homeland Security (DHS) in 2002, which included cybersecurity as a core component of its mission.

The 2010s saw a proliferation of sophisticated cyberattacks, with state-sponsored hacking groups, criminal organizations, and hacktivists all vying for control of cyberspace. Incidents like the Stuxnet worm, attributed to nation-state actors, demonstrated the potential for cyberattacks to disrupt critical infrastructure and even sabotage industrial systems.

Throughout this period, the concept of "ethical hacking" gained prominence. Ethical hackers, often called "white hat" hackers, use their skills to identify and rectify vulnerabilities in systems rather than exploit them. Their role in bolstering cybersecurity became increasingly important, and organizations began to actively employ them to perform penetration testing and security assessments.

Today, in the 21st century, cybersecurity has become an integral part of our digital lives. It encompasses a wide range of technologies and practices, including firewalls, intrusion detection systems, encryption, and multi-factor authentication. The cybersecurity sector has emerged as a result of the enormous amount and complexity of cyber threats, which is projected to continue growing as organizations and governments invest in protecting their digital assets.

The future of cybersecurity holds both promise and challenges. Artificial intelligence (also called AI) and quantum computing are examples of emerging technologies that have the ability to completely change cyberattacks and cyber defense. AI has the potential to detect and react to threats instantly, but quantum computing could jeopardize current encryption techniques. As such, the cat-and-mouse game between defenders and attackers will undoubtedly continue to evolve.

In conclusion, the historical context and evolution of cybersecurity provide a compelling narrative of human ingenuity and the challenges posed by advancing technology. From the early days of computing to the interconnected world we live in today, the need for cybersecurity has never been greater. It is a field that demands constant adaptation and vigilance, as the digital realm continues to shape our lives and societies. As we move forward, cybersecurity will remain a cornerstone of our digital age, safeguarding our data, privacy, and the critical systems upon which we rely.

Importance of cybersecurity in the digital age

The widespread adoption of technology in many facets of our life has brought forth previously unheard-of possibilities for invention, communication, and business in the modern world. However, a new set of threats and problems have also been brought forth by this digital revolution. The significance of cybersecurity has grown as our everyday activities become more and more dependent on digital systems and networks. The many facets of cybersecurity in the digital age will be discussed in this section, along with how it safeguards our data, privacy, economy, vital infrastructure, and national security.

At the heart of the importance of cybersecurity lies the protection of sensitive data. In an era where personal, financial, and medical information is stored electronically and transmitted across vast networks, the potential for data breaches has grown exponentially. These breaches can have severe consequences, leading to identity theft, financial loss, and reputational damage. Moreover, organizations and governments are custodians of massive datasets containing valuable information. Ensuring the confidentiality and integrity of this data is not only a matter of trust but also a legal and ethical responsibility.

Privacy, a fundamental human right, is closely intertwined with cybersecurity. The digital age has blurred the lines between public and private life. We share our thoughts, feelings, and personal details on social media, engage in online shopping, and conduct sensitive transactions over the internet. In this landscape, the importance of protecting our digital privacy cannot be overstated. Cybersecurity safeguards our online identities and ensures that our personal information remains ours alone.

The global economy is another arena profoundly impacted by the importance of cybersecurity. Digital commerce has become the lifeblood of business, enabling transactions on a scale previously unimaginable. However, this interconnected ecosystem is highly susceptible to cyberattacks. Data breaches, ransomware, and financial fraud pose significant threats to businesses, resulting in financial losses, legal liabilities, and damaged customer trust. In essence, the economic prosperity of nations depends on the resilience of their digital infrastructure.

Critical infrastructure, encompassing sectors like energy, healthcare, transportation, and water supply, relies heavily on digital control systems. These systems enhance efficiency and responsiveness but are vulnerable to cyberattacks. The repercussions of a successful attack on critical infrastructure can be catastrophic, disrupting essential services, causing economic turmoil, and potentially endangering lives. The importance of cybersecurity extends to protecting these vital systems from exploitation and manipulation.

In the realm of national security, the significance of cybersecurity has grown exponentially. Nation-states and state-sponsored actors are active participants in the digital battleground, using cyberattacks for espionage, sabotage, and influence campaigns. The growing interconnectivity of military systems, critical infrastructure, and government operations has created a broad attack surface. Thus, a robust cybersecurity posture is essential to safeguarding a nation's sovereignty and ensuring the continuity of government and defense capabilities.

Cybersecurity is not solely a concern for governments and large organizations. Individuals play a crucial role in this ecosystem. From choosing strong passwords to recognizing phishing attempts, the actions of every internet user can either contribute to or compromise cybersecurity. Education and awareness are pivotal in empowering individuals to protect themselves and make informed choices online.

The interconnectedness of our digital world means that cybersecurity is a global concern. Cyber threats transcend borders and can emanate from any corner of the globe. International cooperation and information sharing are vital to combating these threats effectively. Cybersecurity partnerships and agreements between nations have become integral to global security efforts.

As we navigate the digital age, the importance of cybersecurity is continually evolving. New technologies, including AI, the Internet of Things (IoT), and quantum computing, introduce both opportunities and challenges. AI can enhance cyber defenses by identifying threats in real-time, but it can also be exploited by attackers to automate and amplify their attacks. IoT devices, while providing convenience, increase the attack surface, potentially enabling cybercriminals to compromise home networks and systems. Quantum computing, once realized, threatens current encryption methods, necessitating the development of quantum-resistant encryption algorithms.

In conclusion, the significance of cybersecurity in the digital age is multifaceted and far-reaching. It underpins the protection of sensitive data, ensures the preservation of privacy, safeguards the global economy, protects critical infrastructure, and secures national sovereignty. It is a responsibility shared by individuals, organizations, and governments alike. As technology continues to advance, the importance of cybersecurity will only grow, requiring ongoing innovation, education, and international collaboration. It is the shield that enables us to embrace the benefits of the digital age while defending against its inherent risks, ensuring a safer and more secure digital future for all.

CHAPTER II

The Fundamentals of Hacking

What is hacking?

The term "hacking" is a linguistic chameleon, capable of evoking a myriad of images and emotions depending on one's perspective. To some, it represents a nefarious world of digital criminality and cyberattacks, while to others, it embodies the spirit of exploration, innovation, and problem-solving. Hacking, in its essence, is a multifaceted concept that defies a simple, one-size-fits-all definition. In this section, we will unravel the complex nature of hacking, exploring its history, its various forms, the ethical considerations that surround it, and its evolving role in our increasingly digital world.

At its most basic level, hacking can be defined as the process of gaining unauthorized access to computer systems, networks, or data. This definition, however, barely scratches the surface of the intricate tapestry that is hacking. To truly understand hacking, one must delve into its historical roots. Hacking, in the original sense, emerged in the computer laboratories of the 1960s and 1970s. In these early days of computing, hacking was more about curiosity and exploration than malicious intent. Technically astute individuals, often referred to as "hackers," sought to understand and manipulate computer systems, pushing the boundaries of what was possible. Their motivations were rooted in a quest for knowledge and a desire to unlock the secrets of technology.

The term "hacker" itself originally held a positive connotation, referring to those who possessed an innate talent for understanding and modifying systems. These early hackers were the architects of the digital revolution, pioneering concepts such as time-sharing, which laid the groundwork for modern computing. Richard Stallman, a prominent figure in the free software movement, embodies this original spirit of hacking. He once remarked, "To 'hack' is to engage in activities (like programming or other media) in a spirit of playfulness and exploration."

However, as computing technology evolved and society became increasingly reliant on digital systems, the landscape of hacking shifted. Malicious actors began exploiting vulnerabilities for personal gain or to cause harm. This shift led to the coining of terms like "black hat hackers" to describe those with malicious intent and "white hat hackers" for those who used their skills for ethical purposes. The emergence of black hat hacking marked a pivotal moment in the perception of hacking, turning it into a symbol of threat and insecurity.

Yet, hacking has always encompassed a spectrum of activities, ranging from the malicious to the benevolent. Ethical hacking, often called "white hat" hacking, involves individuals who use their technical prowess to identify vulnerabilities and strengthen security. Ethical hackers are vital in safeguarding digital systems, as they proactively identify weaknesses before malicious actors can exploit them. This practice is often associated with penetration testing, vulnerability assessment, and security research.

One of the ethical hacking's most celebrated forms is bug bounty programs. Companies and organizations invite ethical hackers to detect and report vulnerabilities in their software or systems. These programs offer financial rewards, recognition, and, most importantly, the opportunity to contribute to improved cybersecurity. Hackers who engage in bug bounty programs are akin to digital detectives, hunting for vulnerabilities in the digital landscape.

Another facet of hacking that has garnered attention is hacktivism. Hacktivists are individuals or groups who utilize hacking techniques to advance social, political, or environmental causes. While hacktivism can sometimes cross ethical boundaries, it has been instrumental in fostering awareness and promoting change. For example, groups like Anonymous have used their hacking skills to expose corruption and advocate for social justice.

The motivations behind hacking are as diverse as the techniques employed. Some hackers seek financial gain through activities like stealing personal information or cryptocurrency. Others engage in hacking for political reasons, attempting to influence elections or disrupt government operations. Some hackers are driven by ideological beliefs or simply the thrill of the challenge. The motivations of ethical hackers, on the other hand, are rooted in a desire to protect and secure digital systems. As

hacking continues to evolve, ethical considerations come to the forefront. The line between ethical and unethical hacking can be blurry, and what one person views as a noble cause, another might see as a criminal act. Legal and moral boundaries in hacking are continually tested and debated. The question of whether hacking is inherently good or bad remains unresolved, and the answer often depends on one's perspective and the specific actions involved.

In the digital age, hacking has transcended its original domain of computer systems and now encompasses a wide array of targets. Internet of Things (IoT) devices, which include everything from smart refrigerators to industrial control systems, have introduced new opportunities and challenges for hackers. The interconnectedness of these devices presents an expansive attack surface, making security a critical concern.

With the advent of cloud computing and the proliferation of online services, hacking has also expanded to encompass data breaches and privacy violations. Cybercriminals target databases and online platforms to steal sensitive information, often for financial gain or identity theft. These breaches can have severe consequences, affecting individuals, businesses, and even governments.

The future of hacking is closely tied to the evolution of technology itself. As artificial intelligence (AI) and machine learning become more prominent, hackers can leverage these technologies to automate attacks and devise more sophisticated strategies. AI-driven cybersecurity tools are also being developed to combat threats in real-time, creating a digital battlefield where machines are pitted against machines.

The rise of quantum computing presents both opportunities and threats in the world of hacking. Quantum computers have the ability to break existing encryption methods, rendering much of our current cybersecurity infrastructure obsolete. Consequently, researchers are working on quantum-resistant encryption algorithms to protect against this emerging threat.

In conclusion, the concept of hacking is a multifaceted one, with a rich history and a diverse array of motivations and methods. While it has evolved from its innocent origins as a pursuit of knowledge and exploration, hacking remains a powerful force in the digital age. It encompasses both ethical and malicious activities, raising complex ethical and legal questions. As technology advances, the role of hacking will undoubtedly continue to evolve, shaping the digital landscape in ways that are both challenging and transformative. Hacking, for better or worse, is an enduring facet of our increasingly interconnected world.

Different types of hackers (white hat, black hat, grey hat)

The world of hacking is a multifaceted realm, inhabited by a diverse range of individuals with varying motivations and ethical stances. Hackers, often depicted as shadowy figures hunched over computer keyboards, can be broadly categorized into three distinct archetypes: white hat, black hat, and grey hat hackers. Each of these categories represents a unique facet of the hacking subculture, with its own set of principles, practices, and ethical considerations. In this section, we will delve into the fascinating world of hackers, exploring the defining characteristics, motivations, and roles of white hat, black hat, and grey hat hackers in the digital age.

White hat hackers, often called "ethical hackers," are the unsung heroes of the digital world. They use their technical skills and knowledge to uncover vulnerabilities in computer systems, networks, and applications. Unlike their black hat counterparts, white hat hackers operate with the explicit permission of the system owners, aiming to strengthen security rather than exploit weaknesses. Their primary motivation is to protect and defend against cyber threats.

One of the most prominent roles of white hat hackers is in the field of penetration testing, where they systematically attempt to breach the security of an organization's systems to identify weaknesses. This process helps organizations proactively fix vulnerabilities before malicious actors can exploit them. White hat hackers also engage in vulnerability assessment, security auditing, and security research to stay at the forefront of emerging threats and technologies.

Ethical hackers comply to a strict code of ethics, ensuring that their actions are legal and ethical. They seek permission, often through formal agreements like bug bounty programs, before attempting to identify and rectify security flaws. Their objective is not to cause harm or disruption but to fortify the digital defenses of their clients.

Certifications like Certified Ethical Hacker (CEH) and Certified Information Systems Security Professional (CISSP) are highly recognized in the field of ethical hacking. These certifications verify the skills and knowledge of white hat hackers and are often prerequisites for employment in cybersecurity roles.

White hat hackers play an indispensable role in safeguarding digital systems, contributing to the overall security of the digital age. Their actions ensure that vulnerabilities are addressed promptly, reducing the risk of cyberattacks as well as data breaches. Their work is guided by a commitment to ethical principles and a mission to make cyberspace a safer place for all.

In stark contrast to white hat hackers, black hat hackers are often portrayed as the antagonists of the digital realm. They engage in hacking activities with malicious intent, seeking to exploit vulnerabilities for personal gain or to cause harm. Their motivations can range from financial profit to political activism, and their actions are frequently illegal.

Financial gain is a potent motivator for many black hat hackers. Cybercrime, including activities like identity theft, credit card fraud, and ransomware attacks, has become a lucrative industry. These hackers often target individuals, businesses, and financial institutions, seeking to steal sensitive data or extort money through various means.

State-sponsored hacking is another prominent category within the black hat hacker domain. Nation-states and intelligence agencies engage in cyber espionage, cyber warfare, and influence operations, using hacking techniques to gather intelligence, disrupt critical infrastructure, or influence political events. These state-sponsored actors operate with the backing of their governments and have access to significant resources and expertise.

Hacktivism is a subset of black hat hacking motivated by political or social causes. Hacktivists aim to advance their ideologies or draw attention to specific issues through hacking activities. Groups like Anonymous have gained notoriety for their hacktivist actions, often targeting government websites and organizations associated with controversial policies.

Black hat hackers are not confined to a single geographical location or demographic. They operate across the globe, and their actions can have far-reaching consequences. Their disregard for legal and ethical boundaries makes them a significant challenge for law enforcement and cybersecurity professionals.

Grey hat hackers, as the name suggests, occupy a nebulous middle ground between the ethical white hats and the malicious black hats. They engage in hacking activities without explicit authorization but often without the intent to cause harm. Grey hat hackers may discover vulnerabilities in systems and disclose them to the affected parties, but they do so without obtaining permission beforehand.

One defining characteristic of grey hat hackers is their ambiguous ethical stance. They believe they are acting in the best interest of security, often arguing that their actions are necessary to highlight vulnerabilities and encourage system owners to address them. However, their methods can raise ethical and legal questions, as they may involve unauthorized access to systems and data.

Grey hat hackers have been responsible for uncovering critical vulnerabilities in widely utilized software and systems. They often choose to disclose their findings to the public or the affected organizations, sometimes after a responsible disclosure period has passed. While their intentions may be noble, their actions can create tension between security researchers, software vendors, and the legal system.

The motivations of grey hat hackers vary. Some are genuinely driven by a desire to improve cybersecurity and protect users from potential harm. Others may seek recognition within the hacking community or the possibility of financial rewards, similar to ethical hackers who participate in bug bounty programs.

Their actions walk a fine line between ethical and unethical hacking, and the perception of grey hat hacking can be polarized. Some view them as whistleblowers who expose vulnerabilities that would otherwise remain hidden, while others consider their unauthorized actions as unacceptable.

In the digital age, hacking has evolved into a complex and multifaceted landscape, with white hat, black hat, and grey hat hackers each representing distinct aspects of this realm. White hat hackers are the ethical guardians, striving to protect digital systems and data. Black hat hackers, on the other hand, exploit vulnerabilities for personal gain or harm, often engaging in cybercrime or state-sponsored hacking. Grey hat hackers occupy an ambiguous middle ground, conducting unauthorized activities with the intention of improving security but raising ethical and legal questions.

Hacking is a domain where the boundaries between good and bad are often blurred, and the motivations and actions of hackers span a wide spectrum. Ethical considerations play a central role in defining the role of hackers within this landscape. As the digital world continues to evolve, the actions and impact of hackers will continue to shape the security of our interconnected society, making it essential to understand and navigate the diverse landscape of hacking in the digital age.

The ethics of hacking

In the ever-evolving landscape of technology and cyberspace, the concept of hacking stands as both a testament to human ingenuity and a source of significant ethical quandaries. Hacking, the act of getting unauthorized access to computer systems, networks, or data, has been both celebrated as a tool for innovation and vilified as a means of exploitation. To fully understand the ethics of hacking, one must delve into the multifaceted world of hacking practices, motivations, and the moral dilemmas that accompany them. In this section, we will explore the ethical considerations surrounding hacking, examine the various ethical frameworks applied to this complex field, and discuss the critical role of ethical hacking in securing our digital world.

Hacking, as a term, encompasses a wide spectrum of activities, each with its own ethical implications. On one end of the spectrum, ethical hacking, often referred to as "white hat" hacking, embodies the highest moral standards within the hacking community. Ethical hackers use their technical skills and knowledge to identify vulnerabilities and strengthen security systems, typically with the consent of system owners. Their primary goal is to protect digital systems and data, and their actions are governed by a strong commitment to ethics and legality.

In contrast, black hat hackers, often depicted as the dark side of hacking, operate with malicious intent. They seek to exploit vulnerabilities for personal gain, whether it be financial profit, political influence, or pure mischief. Their actions are frequently illegal and unethical, causing harm to individuals, businesses, and governments. Black hat hackers occupy the extreme end of the ethical spectrum, engaging in activities that are universally condemned.

Between these two extremes lies the realm of grey hat hackers. Grey hat hackers conduct hacking activities without explicit authorization but often with the intent to uncover and disclose vulnerabilities. While their motivations may be rooted in security concerns, their actions raise ethical and legal questions. They operate in an ambiguous middle ground, navigating the tension between the pursuit of knowledge and the respect for legal boundaries.

The ethical considerations surrounding hacking are often guided by various ethical frameworks and principles. One of the most prominent frameworks is utilitarianism, which evaluates actions based on their overall utility or benefit to society. From a utilitarian perspective, ethical hacking can be justified as it ultimately contributes to improved cybersecurity and protects society from cyber threats. Black hat hacking, on the other hand, is seen as detrimental to society, causing harm and chaos.

Deontological ethics, another significant framework, focuses on the inherent morality of actions rather than their consequences. From a deontological standpoint, the act of hacking without authorization is inherently unethical, as it violates the principle of respecting property rights and laws. Ethical hacking aligns with deontological ethics when conducted with the permission of system owners, as it adheres to principles of consent and legal compliance.

Virtue ethics, which emphasizes the development of virtuous character traits, plays a role in the ethical considerations of hacking. Ethical hackers often embody virtues such as honesty, responsibility, and integrity, aligning with the tenets of virtue ethics. Black hat hackers, in contrast, may embody vices such as deceit, recklessness, and malicious intent, which are contrary to virtuous character traits.

A relatively recent ethical framework that has gained prominence in the context of hacking is hacker ethics. Hacker ethics, as articulated by figures like Steven Levy in his book "Hackers: Heroes of the Computer Revolution," emphasize values such as the pursuit of knowledge, the free exchange of information, and the challenge of authority. From this perspective, ethical hackers embody the true spirit of hacking, as they seek to expand knowledge and promote security. However, hacker ethics also acknowledge the potential for harm in hacking, emphasizing the importance of responsible and ethical hacking practices.

Ethical hacking, often referred to as the "good side" of hacking, is a critical component of the ethical considerations surrounding hacking. Ethical hackers, often called white hat hackers, play a pivotal role in safeguarding digital systems and networks. They proactively identify vulnerabilities, report them to system owners, and work to rectify weaknesses before malicious actors can exploit them.

The practice of ethical hacking includes a wide range of activities, such as penetration testing, vulnerability assessment, security auditing, and security research. Organizations often engage ethical hackers to assess the security of their systems, conduct security audits, and participate in bug bounty programs. These activities help organizations identify and address vulnerabilities, mitigating the risk of cyberattacks and data breaches.

Certifications like Certified Ethical Hacker (CEH) and Certified Information Systems Security Professional (CISSP) validate the skills and knowledge of ethical hackers, providing a structured path for individuals seeking to enter the field. Ethical hacking is a recognized and respected profession within the cybersecurity community, and ethical hackers are valued for their contributions to digital security.

The ethical dilemmas faced by ethical hackers are complex and multifaceted. They must navigate legal boundaries, respect privacy rights, and take into account the potential impact of their actions on the systems they assess. Responsible disclosure of vulnerabilities is a critical aspect of ethical hacking, ensuring that system owners have the opportunity to address security flaws before they are publicly disclosed.

The ethics of hacking is a nuanced and developing field, shaped by a complex interplay of motivations, actions, and ethical frameworks. Hacking spans a wide spectrum of activities, from ethical hacking that aims to protect digital systems to black hat hacking driven by malicious intent. Grey hat hackers operate in an ambiguous middle ground, conducting unauthorized activities with varying ethical justifications.

Ethical considerations in hacking are guided by ethical frameworks such as utilitarianism, deontological ethics, virtue ethics, and hacker ethics. These frameworks provide a foundation for evaluating the morality of hacking actions, whether they align with societal values and principles.

Ethical hacking, as a practice, is the embodiment of responsible and moral hacking. Ethical hackers contribute to the security of digital systems by identifying vulnerabilities and collaborating with system owners to address them. They comply to a stringent code of ethics, emphasizing legality, consent, and the pursuit of knowledge.

In the digital age, where cyber threats are pervasive, ethical hacking serves as a moral imperative. It helps protect individuals, organizations, and society at large from the ever-present risks of cyberattacks and data breaches. The role of ethical hackers in securing our digital world cannot be overstated, and their actions reflect the ethical responsibility to safeguard the interconnected systems upon which we rely.

CHAPTER III

Ethical Hacking vs. Unethical Hacking

Defining ethical hacking

In the vast and ever-evolving landscape of cybersecurity, where threats loom large and the digital realm is rife with vulnerabilities, the concept of ethical hacking emerges as a beacon of light amidst the darkness. Ethical hacking, often called "white hat" hacking, is a practice that embodies a paradox: it is the art of hacking for good, the act of penetrating computer systems, networks, and applications with the explicit intent of identifying and rectifying security flaws. This seemingly contradictory pursuit lies at the heart of ethical hacking, a discipline that is fundamentally rooted in principles of knowledge, responsibility, and ethical conduct. In this section, we will delve into the intricacies of defining ethical hacking, exploring its purpose, methodologies, ethical considerations, and its indispensable role in the modern digital landscape.

At its core, ethical hacking is driven by a noble purpose—
to safeguard digital systems, data, and networks from malicious cyber threats. It is the proactive quest to identify vulnerabilities before malicious actors can exploit them. Ethical hackers, like digital sentinels, use their technical skills and knowledge to penetrate systems and applications, exposing security weaknesses that might otherwise remain hidden. Their mission is clear: to protect the digital world from the ever-present dangers of cyberattacks, data breaches, and online vulnerabilities.

Ethical hacking is not a malevolent endeavor; it is a constructive and preventive one. The ultimate goal is not to cause harm but to strengthen security, to fortify the digital defenses that protect organizations, governments, and individuals alike. Ethical hackers operate with a sense of responsibility, knowing that their actions can have far-reaching consequences in an increasingly interconnected world.

Ethical hacking encompasses a broad range of methodologies and techniques, each carefully tailored to uncover specific vulnerabilities. These methodologies are meticulously planned, executed, and documented, following a structured approach that mirrors the modus operandi of malicious hackers. The primary objective is to simulate real-world attack scenarios, revealing potential weak points in a system's defenses.

One of the fundamental techniques employed by ethical hackers is penetration testing. Penetration testing involves a systematic evaluation of a system's security by attempting to exploit vulnerabilities. It encompasses various levels, including network penetration testing, web application penetration testing, and also wireless network penetration testing. Ethical hackers leverage their knowledge to launch simulated attacks, mimicking the actions of malicious hackers to uncover potential weaknesses.

Vulnerability assessment is another crucial aspect of ethical hacking. It involves the identification and assessment of vulnerabilities within systems, applications, and networks. Ethical hackers use specialized tools and methodologies to scan for vulnerabilities, rate their severity, and provide recommendations for remediation. The goal is not only to identify weaknesses but also to prioritize them based on their potential impact and exploitability.

Ethical hackers also engage in security auditing, a comprehensive examination of an organization's security policies, procedures, and controls. Security audits aim to assess compliance with security standards, identify policy gaps, and recommend improvements. By scrutinizing an organization's security posture from a holistic perspective, ethical hackers help ensure that all aspects of security are addressed.

Security research plays a pivotal role in the world of ethical hacking. Ethical hackers continuously explore new attack vectors, vulnerabilities, and exploits. They contribute to the cybersecurity community by publishing their findings, which often lead to the development of patches, security updates, and best practices. The cycle of research, discovery, and remediation is fundamental to the ongoing evolution of ethical hacking.

Ethical hacking operates within a framework of stringent ethical considerations, reflecting a commitment to responsible and lawful conduct. Key ethical principles guide the actions of ethical hackers, ensuring that their activities align with societal values and legal boundaries.

One of the paramount ethical principles in ethical hacking is legality. Ethical hackers operate within the confines of the law, seeking explicit permission from system owners or authorized parties before conducting assessments.

This ensures that their actions are not only ethical but also lawful, avoiding potential legal repercussions.

Informed consent is another ethical cornerstone. Ethical hackers obtain explicit consent from system owners or administrators before initiating assessments. Informed consent ensures that the stakeholders are aware of the hacking activities and have agreed to them voluntarily. It underscores the principle of respecting individuals' autonomy and decisions regarding their digital assets.

The principle of responsible disclosure is integral to ethical hacking. When ethical hackers identify vulnerabilities, they follow a responsible disclosure process, which involves notifying system owners or software vendors and allowing them a reasonable amount of time to address and remediate the issues. Responsible disclosure prevents the premature public disclosure of vulnerabilities, giving organizations the opportunity to protect their systems before potential exploitation.

Privacy considerations are vital in ethical hacking. Ethical hackers are acutely aware of privacy rights and data protection regulations. They take measures to minimize the collection and retention of personal data during assessments and ensure that any data accessed or obtained is handled with the utmost care and confidentiality.

Transparency and accountability are fundamental ethical principles. Ethical hackers maintain transparency by fully documenting their actions, methodologies, and findings. This documentation serves as a record of their activities and provides a clear audit trail for system owners and stakeholders. Accountability ensures that ethical hackers are responsible for the consequences of their actions and any recommendations or advice provided.

In the modern digital landscape, the role of ethical hacking is indispensable. Cyber threats continue to evolve and adapt, exploiting vulnerabilities that emerge as technology advances. Ethical hackers stand as the first line of defense, tirelessly working to identify and mitigate these vulnerabilities before they can be utilized by malicious actors.

Organizations and governments around the world recognize the value of ethical hacking and often engage ethical hackers to evaluate the security of their digital assets. Bug bounty programs, which offer financial rewards for the responsible disclosure of vulnerabilities, incentivize ethical hackers to uncover weaknesses and report them promptly.

Ethical hacking is not limited to the private sector. Governments and law enforcement agencies employ ethical hackers to protect critical infrastructure, national security, and sensitive information. Ethical hackers play a crucial role in defending against cyber threats that can have far-reaching consequences, including attacks on power grids, financial systems, and communication networks.

Furthermore, ethical hacking is a dynamic field, constantly evolving to adapt to emerging technologies and threats. As AI, the Internet of Things (IoT), and quantum computing become more prominent, ethical hackers are at the forefront of identifying and addressing the security challenges posed by these innovations. They are instrumental in developing and implementing new security measures and best practices to safeguard the digital future.

Ethical hacking, the art of hacking for good, stands as a beacon of ethical conduct in the digital realm. It is a practice rooted in the pursuit of knowledge, responsibility, and ethical principles. Ethical hackers employ a range of methodologies to uncover vulnerabilities, all the while adhering to strict ethical considerations that emphasize legality, informed consent, responsible disclosure, privacy, transparency, and accountability.

In the digital age, where cyber threats loom large, ethical hacking plays an indispensable role. Ethical hackers are the guardians of the digital world, tirelessly working to identify and mitigate vulnerabilities before they can be utilized by malicious actors. Their contributions are pivotal in protecting individuals, organizations, and governments from the ever-present dangers of cyberattacks and data breaches.

Ethical hacking is not just a profession; it is a moral imperative. It embodies the ethical responsibility to safeguard the interconnected systems upon which society relies. As technology advances, the role of ethical hacking will remain essential, ensuring that the digital landscape remains a secure and resilient domain for all.

Contrasting ethical hacking with malicious hacking

In the labyrinthine world of hacking, where digital borders blur and lines between right and wrong often appear nebulous, two distinct archetypes emerge: ethical hackers and malicious hackers. These two groups represent radically divergent goals, values, and effects on the digital sphere, and they are at the extremes of the ethical spectrum. Ethical hackers, often referred to as "white hat" hackers, are the digital sentinels who wield their technical prowess for the greater good, probing systems and networks to uncover vulnerabilities before malicious actors can exploit them. In stark contrast, malicious hackers, known as "black hat" hackers, operate with malevolent intent, seeking to exploit weaknesses for personal gain, disruption, or harm. This section aims to illuminate the stark contrasts between ethical hacking and malicious hacking, exploring their motivations, methodologies, ethical considerations, and the consequential impact they have on the cybersecurity landscape.

The motivations that drive individuals toward ethical hacking or malicious hacking are as disparate as the outcomes they seek. Ethical hackers, driven by a sense of responsibility and a commitment to protecting digital systems, dedicate their skills to fortifying cybersecurity. Their primary aim is to safeguard organizations, individuals, and critical infrastructure from the incessant barrage of cyber threats.

Conversely, malicious hackers operate in pursuit of personal gain or gratification. Their motivations range from financial profit and data theft to political activism or simply the thrill of causing disruption. For some, hacking is a means of acquiring illicit wealth through activities like identity theft, ransomware attacks, or credit card fraud. Others may be ideologically motivated, using hacking to further political or social causes, often engaging in hacktivism.

The motivations of malicious hackers are not confined to personal gain. Nation-states and state-sponsored hackers employ malicious hacking techniques for espionage, sabotage, and influence campaigns. In this realm, hacking becomes a tool for geopolitical maneuvering and intelligence gathering.

Ethical hackers and malicious hackers employ vastly different methodologies in their pursuits. Ethical hacking embraces a systematic, responsible, and consent-driven approach, while malicious hacking is often marked by covert, unauthorized, and illicit activities.

Ethical hackers engage in a wide array of activities designed to identify and rectify vulnerabilities. Penetration testing, one of the core methodologies, involves systematic attempts to breach the security of systems and networks. Vulnerability assessment, security auditing, and responsible disclosure are integral components of ethical hacking, emphasizing legality, informed consent, and transparency.

Malicious hackers, on the other hand, rely on unauthorized access and exploitation. They often exploit vulnerabilities without consent, employing techniques that are illegal and unethical. The actions of malicious hackers include infiltrating systems to steal sensitive data, launching distributed denial of service (DDoS) attacks to disrupt services, or deploying malware to compromise devices.

A defining aspect of ethical hacking is its commitment to responsible disclosure. Ethical hackers identify vulnerabilities and promptly notify system owners or vendors to facilitate remediation. This practice minimizes the risk of harm and ensures that security weaknesses are addressed before they can be exploited.

In contrast, malicious hackers often weaponize vulnerabilities, leveraging them for personal gain or to inflict harm on targeted individuals, organizations, or governments. The methods employed by malicious hackers can vary widely, from social engineering tactics to exploit kits and zero-day vulnerabilities.

The ethical considerations that guide ethical hacking and malicious hacking are perhaps the most pronounced distinctions between the two. Ethical hacking operates within a framework of stringent ethical principles that emphasize legality, informed consent, responsible disclosure, privacy, transparency, and accountability.

Legality is a fundamental ethical principle in ethical hacking. Ethical hackers operate within the bounds of the law, seeking explicit permission from system owners or authorized parties before conducting assessments. This ensures that their actions are not only ethical but also compliant with legal standards.

Informed consent underscores the principle of respecting individuals' autonomy and decisions regarding their digital assets. Ethical hackers obtain explicit consent from system owners or administrators before initiating assessments, ensuring that stakeholders are aware of the hacking activities and have agreed to them voluntarily.

Responsible disclosure is integral to ethical hacking. Ethical hackers follow a responsible disclosure process, notifying system owners or software vendors and allowing them a reasonable amount of time to address and remediate vulnerabilities. This prevents the premature public disclosure of vulnerabilities, giving organizations the opportunity to protect their systems before potential exploitation.

Privacy considerations are vital in ethical hacking. Ethical hackers are acutely aware of privacy rights and data protection regulations. They take measures to minimize the collection and retention of personal data during assessments, ensuring that any data accessed or obtained is handled with care and confidentiality.

Transparency and accountability are fundamental ethical principles that govern ethical hacking. Ethical hackers maintain transparency by fully documenting their actions, methodologies, and findings. This documentation serves as a record of their activities and provides a clear audit trail for system owners and stakeholders. Accountability ensures that ethical hackers are responsible for the consequences of their actions and any recommendations or advice provided.

In contrast, malicious hacking operates in ethical and legal gray areas. Malicious hackers often engage in activities that are both unethical and illegal, violating principles of legality, informed consent, responsible disclosure, privacy, transparency, and accountability. Their actions are characterized by secrecy and evasion, evading law enforcement while seeking to exploit vulnerabilities for personal gain or to inflict harm.

The consequences and impact of ethical hacking and malicious hacking are profound and far-reaching, affecting individuals, organizations, governments, and society as a whole. Ethical hacking contributes to a safer and more secure digital landscape, helping organizations and governments protect critical infrastructure, sensitive data, and individual privacy.

Ethical hackers serve as digital sentinels, identifying and rectifying vulnerabilities that could otherwise be exploited by malicious hackers. Their work bolsters cybersecurity, reduces the risk of cyberattacks and data breaches, and safeguards the integrity of digital systems.

Organizations and governments acknowledge the value of ethical hacking and often engage ethical hackers to assess the security of their digital assets. Bug bounty programs, which offer financial rewards for the responsible disclosure of vulnerabilities, incentivize ethical hackers to uncover weaknesses and report them promptly.

Malicious hacking, in stark contrast, inflicts harm and disruption upon digital landscapes. The actions of malicious hackers can result in financial losses, reputational damage, legal liabilities, and the compromise of sensitive information.

Cyberattacks orchestrated by malicious hackers can have severe consequences, ranging from the theft of personal and financial data to the disruption of critical infrastructure. Ransomware attacks, for example, can cripple businesses and organizations, leading to financial extortion and data loss. DDoS attacks can render websites and services inaccessible, causing inconvenience and economic losses.

State-sponsored malicious hacking can escalate international tensions and lead to cyber warfare, with governments targeting each other's critical infrastructure and engaging in cyber espionage. The repercussions of such actions can be far-reaching and impact global security.

Ethical hacking and malicious hacking represent two fundamentally divergent paths within the world of hacking. Ethical hackers, driven by responsibility and ethical considerations, are the defenders of the digital realm, working diligently to safeguard systems, networks, and data. They adhere to strict ethical principles, ensuring that their actions align with societal values and legal standards.

In contrast, malicious hackers operate with malevolent intent, seeking personal gain, disruption, or harm. Their actions often breach ethical and legal boundaries, causing harm to individuals, organizations, and governments.

The distinctions between ethical hacking and malicious hacking are clear and pronounced, encompassing motivations, methodologies, ethical considerations, and consequences. A world that is becoming more interconnected, where cyber threats persist and technology evolves, the role of ethical hacking remains indispensable, serving as a bulwark against the ever-present dangers of cyberattacks and data breaches. It is a testament to the ethical imperative of protecting the digital landscape upon which society relies.

Legal and ethical considerations in ethical hacking

In the intricate world of ethical hacking, where security professionals strive to protect digital landscapes from malicious actors, the importance of legal and ethical considerations cannot be overstated. Ethical hackers, often referred to as "white hat" hackers, operate under a framework that values responsible conduct and compliance with the law. Their mission is to uncover vulnerabilities, bolster cybersecurity, and safeguard digital systems. However, their actions are governed by a strict set of ethical principles and legal boundaries that define the parameters of their work. In this section, we will delve into the legal and ethical considerations that guide ethical hacking, exploring the principles of legality, informed consent, responsible disclosure, privacy, transparency, and accountability that underpin this essential discipline.

Perhaps the most fundamental legal consideration in ethical hacking is operating within the boundaries of the law. Ethical hackers must ensure that their actions are compliant with local, national, and international laws and regulations. This requirement extends to all aspects of their work, from obtaining consent for assessments to responsibly disclosing vulnerabilities.

Operating within the confines of the law is essential to avoid legal repercussions that can have severe consequences. Unauthorized hacking activities, even if conducted with benevolent intent, can still lead to criminal charges and penalties. Thus, ethical hackers must seek explicit permission from system owners or authorized parties before conducting assessments, ensuring that their actions are both ethical and lawful.

Legal considerations also apply to the handling of data and information obtained during assessments. Ethical hackers must be aware of data protection laws and privacy regulations, ensuring that any data accessed or obtained is handled in accordance with legal standards. Failure to do so can lead to privacy violations and legal liabilities.

Informed permission is a fundamental ethical principle that underscores the importance of respecting individuals' autonomy and decisions regarding their digital assets. Ethical hackers must obtain explicit consent from system owners or administrators before initiating assessments. Informed consent ensures that stakeholders are aware of the hacking activities and have agreed to them voluntarily.

In many places, obtaining informed permission is not only the law, but also an ethical obligation. It guarantees that all parties involved are mindful of the possible threats and advantages associated with the evaluation and acts as a precaution against unauthorized hacking.

Informed consent extends beyond the initiation of assessments. Ethical hackers must maintain open lines of communication with system owners or authorized representatives throughout the assessment process, providing regular updates on progress and findings. This transparency ensures that all stakeholders remain informed and can make informed decisions regarding the security of their digital assets.

Responsible disclosure is an integral aspect of ethical hacking, emphasizing the ethical and legal obligation to report vulnerabilities promptly and responsibly. When ethical hackers identify vulnerabilities during assessments, they follow a responsible disclosure process, which involves notifying system owners or software vendors and allowing them a reasonable amount of time to address and remediate the issues.

Responsible disclosure serves multiple purposes. It mitigates the risk of harm by ensuring that vulnerabilities are not prematurely disclosed to the public or malicious actors. It provides system owners with the opportunity to protect their systems and data before potential exploitation occurs. Additionally, it fosters collaboration between ethical hackers and system owners, promoting a shared commitment to cybersecurity.

Failure to adhere to responsible disclosure practices can have ethical and legal implications. Premature or public disclosure of vulnerabilities without giving system owners adequate time to address them can lead to security breaches and legal disputes. Responsible disclosure is, therefore, an ethical imperative that upholds the principles of transparency and collaboration.

Privacy considerations are paramount in ethical hacking. Ethical hackers must be acutely aware of privacy rights and data protection regulations, ensuring that their actions minimize the collection and retention of personal data during assessments.

Protecting sensitive information is not only an ethical duty but also a legal requirement in many jurisdictions. Ethical hackers must take measures to anonymize or pseudonymize data whenever possible and handle any personal or sensitive data with care and confidentiality.

Privacy also extends to the ethical hacker's own actions. Ethical hackers must respect the privacy and confidentiality of any data they access or obtain during assessments, refraining from unauthorized disclosure or misuse. Breaches of privacy can lead to legal liabilities and reputational damage, underscoring the importance of ethical conduct in handling sensitive information.

Transparency is a fundamental ethical principle that governs ethical hacking. Ethical hackers must maintain transparency by fully documenting their actions, methodologies, and findings throughout the assessment process. This documentation serves as a record of their activities and provides a clear audit trail for system owners and stakeholders.

Comprehensive documentation is not only an ethical practice but also a means of ensuring accountability. It allows all parties involved to review the assessment process, understand the steps taken, and assess the validity of the findings. Transparency fosters trust and confidence in the ethical hacking process, promoting collaboration and accountability.

Accountability is another key ethical principle that ethical hackers must uphold. It ensures that ethical hackers are responsible for the consequences of their actions and any recommendations or advice provided. Accountability extends to all aspects of the assessment process, from obtaining informed consent to responsibly disclosing vulnerabilities.

Ethical hackers must be prepared to take responsibility for the impact of their assessments, which may include system downtime, temporary disruption of services, or the discovery of sensitive vulnerabilities. Accountability requires ethical hackers to collaborate with system owners to address and remediate vulnerabilities promptly.

In cases where legal or ethical boundaries are in question, ethical hackers must be prepared to defend their actions and decisions, demonstrating that their conduct aligns with ethical principles and legal standards.

Legal and ethical considerations are the cornerstones of ethical hacking, shaping the principles and practices that guide this essential discipline. Operating within the boundaries of the law, respecting informed consent, adhering to responsible disclosure practices, safeguarding privacy, maintaining transparency, and upholding accountability are the ethical imperatives that govern ethical hacking.

In the intricate dance between legality and ethics, ethical hackers bear the responsibility of safeguarding digital systems, networks, and data while upholding the highest standards of ethical conduct. Their commitment to responsible and lawful hacking contributes to a safer and a more secure digital landscape, protecting individuals, organizations, and governments from the ever-present dangers of cyberattacks and data breaches.

As technology advances and cyber threats evolve, the role of legal and ethical considerations in ethical hacking remains paramount. It is a testament to the ethical imperative of securing the interconnected systems upon which society relies, and a reminder that ethical hacking stands as a bulwark against the darkness of malicious hacking in the digital age.

CHAPTER IV

Cyber Threats and Vulnerabilities

Common cyber threats (viruses, malware, phishing, etc.)

In today's digital age, the realm of cyberspace is teeming with opportunities and innovations, but it is also fraught with peril. A multitude of cyber threats lurk in the shadows, endangering individuals, organizations, and governments alike. These threats are not confined to a single form but encompass a diverse array of malicious activities and tactics. In this section, we will delve into some of the most common cyber threats, shedding light on viruses, malware, phishing, ransomware, and distributed denial of service (DDoS) attacks. By understanding these threats, we can better equip ourselves to defend against them and navigate the complex digital landscape securely.

Viruses represent one of the earliest and most enduring forms of cyber threats. These malicious programs are designed to infect computer systems and replicate themselves, often with the intent of causing harm or disruption. Viruses can attach themselves to legitimate files or software, and when executed, they carry out their malicious actions.

The primary goal of a virus is to compromise the integrity and functionality of a computer system. It can corrupt or delete files, steal sensitive information, or even render the system inoperable. The most common ways that viruses spread are through contaminated removable media, malicious downloads, and infected email attachments.

Over time, the sophistication of viruses has grown significantly. Modern antivirus software and security measures have made it more challenging for viruses to infiltrate systems, but the threat persists. Virus creators continually adapt and evolve their tactics to bypass security defenses and infiltrate vulnerable systems.

Malicious software, malware for short, is a general term for a wide range of dangerous software intended to compromise, corrupt, or access computer systems without authorization. Malware includes viruses, Trojans, worms, spyware, adware, and more. What sets malware apart is its versatility, as it can serve a range of nefarious purposes.

Trojans, for example, are disguised as legitimate software or files, tricking users into installing them. Once inside a system, Trojans can grant remote access to malicious actors or steal sensitive information. Worms are self-replicating malware that can spread rapidly across networks, causing widespread damage.

Spyware and adware, on the other hand, are often used for covert surveillance or advertising purposes, respectively. They can monitor a user's online activities, collect personal information, or inundate a system with unwanted ads.

Malware is frequently spread through deceptive email attachments, compromised websites, or infected downloads. To combat malware, individuals and organizations employ a range of cybersecurity tools, including antivirus software, firewalls, and intrusion detection systems.

Phishing is a cyber threat that preys on human psychology, relying on deception and social engineering to trick individuals into disclosing sensitive data or performing actions that compromise security. Phishing attacks typically involve fraudulent emails, messages, or websites that impersonate trusted entities.

In a phishing attack, the attacker masquerades as a legitimate organization, like a bank, government agency, or reputable company. The message often contains urgent or enticing language, urging the recipient to take immediate action, such as clicking on a link or providing login credentials.

Once the victim falls for the deception and complies with the attacker's request, sensitive information like usernames, passwords, credit card numbers, or personal data is exposed. Phishing attacks can lead to identity theft, financial fraud, or unauthorized access to accounts.

Phishing attacks continue to evolve, with spear-phishing and whaling attacks targeting specific individuals, such as high-profile executives or employees with access to valuable corporate data. To combat phishing, user education, email filtering, and multi-factor authentication are commonly employed security measures.

Ransomware is a particularly insidious form of cyber threat that has gained notoriety in recent years. Malware of this kind encrypts the data of its victims, making it unreadable, and then demands a ransom—typically in cryptocurrency—for the decryption key.

If a ransomware attack is successful, the results could be disastrous. Individuals and organizations may find themselves locked out of critical data, facing financial losses, and grappling with the ethical dilemma of whether to pay the ransom. Payment, however, does not guarantee the safe recovery of data, as attackers are not bound by any code of ethics.

Ransomware attacks often target businesses, healthcare providers, and government agencies, where the loss of data can have severe consequences. These attacks can be delivered through infected email attachments, malicious downloads, or vulnerabilities in software and systems.

To defend against ransomware, robust backup strategies, regular software updates, and employee training are crucial. It is essential to have backup copies of critical data to restore operations in case of an attack and to resist paying ransoms, as it only fuels the ransomware ecosystem.

Distributed Denial of Service, often called DDoS attacks are a form of cyber threat that aims to disrupt the normal functioning of websites, networks, or online services by overwhelming them with an excessive volume of traffic. Attackers use a network of compromised devices, often called a botnet, to flood a target with traffic until it becomes unreachable.

The effect of a successful DDoS attack can be widespread, leading to website downtime, service unavailability, and financial losses. DDoS attacks are often used as a diversionary tactic, distracting security teams from other malicious activities while the attack is ongoing.

One notable characteristic of DDoS attacks is their sheer scale. Attackers leverage numerous compromised devices, which can include computers, IoT devices, or even smartphones, to generate a massive volume of traffic. This makes mitigation challenging and requires specialized DDoS protection measures.

To defend against DDoS attacks, organizations can employ traffic filtering, load balancing, and content delivery networks (CDNs) to absorb excess traffic. Additionally, proactive monitoring and incident response plans are essential to minimize the impact of DDoS attacks.

The digital landscape is fraught with peril, and cyber threats constantly evolve in complexity and scale. Viruses, malware, phishing, ransomware, and DDoS attacks are just a few of the common threats that individuals, organizations, and governments must contend with.

Defending against these threats requires a multifaceted approach, encompassing cybersecurity tools, user education, regular software updates, and a proactive security posture. In an interconnected world where digital assets are increasingly valuable, vigilance and preparedness are paramount to staying one step ahead of cyber adversaries.

By understanding the nature of these common cyber threats and the tactics employed by malicious actors, individuals and organizations can better protect themselves in the complex and ever-changing landscape of cyberspace. It is a constant battle, but with the right knowledge and security measures, it is a battle that can be won.

Identifying vulnerabilities in systems

In today's digital age, where the battle between cybersecurity professionals and malicious actors rages on, identifying vulnerabilities stands as a linchpin of defense. These vulnerabilities, often termed "weaknesses" or "security flaws," represent the Achilles' heels of computer systems, networks, and software applications. They offer entry points for attackers, potential weaknesses that can be exploited to compromise digital assets' security and integrity. In this section, we will explore the profound significance of identifying vulnerabilities in systems, the diverse methods and techniques employed for vulnerability assessment, and the pivotal role this process plays in safeguarding against a multitude of cyber threats.

The identification of vulnerabilities is not merely a best practice; it is the cornerstone of effective cybersecurity. In a digital landscape teeming with cyber threats, from malware to phishing attacks and beyond, knowing where potential weaknesses lie is fundamental to fortifying defenses. Vulnerabilities, if left undetected and unaddressed, can serve as entry points for cybercriminals, enabling them to gain unauthorized access, steal sensitive information, disrupt services, or compromise system integrity.

Furthermore, as technology advances and systems grow more complex, the attack surface—areas vulnerable to exploitation—continues to expand. New software vulnerabilities emerge, and existing ones evolve, making ongoing vulnerability assessment a necessity. Identifying vulnerabilities is not a one-time endeavor but an ongoing process that aligns with the dynamic nature of cybersecurity.

Moreover, vulnerability assessment plays a critical role in compliance with cybersecurity standards and regulations. Many industries, such as finance, healthcare, and critical infrastructure, are subject to stringent cybersecurity requirements. Identifying and mitigating vulnerabilities is a fundamental component of meeting these regulatory mandates.

Vulnerability assessment encompasses a wide array of methods and techniques, each tailored to uncover specific weaknesses in systems, networks, or applications. These methods include automated scanning tools, manual testing, and expert analysis.

Automated scanning tools rapidly and comprehensively assess systems for known vulnerabilities, comparing them against vast databases of known vulnerabilities and associated patches. Manual testing involves human expertise and intuition to identify vulnerabilities that automated tools may miss, requiring skilled security professionals to actively probe systems. Code review examines the source code of software applications line by line, searching for coding errors and insecure practices. Configuration review assesses the settings and configurations of systems and networks, ensuring they adhere to best practices. Threat modeling identifies potential threats and vulnerabilities in the design phase of a system or application. Social engineering tests manipulate individuals within an organization to gain access or information. Finally, wireless network testing evaluates the security of wireless networks, which have become pervasive in the digital era.

Identifying vulnerabilities is not a standalone activity but an integral part of an extensive cybersecurity strategy. Once vulnerabilities are identified, they must be prioritized based on factors such as their potential impact, exploitability, and criticality. This prioritization helps organizations allocate their resources efficiently to address the most pressing vulnerabilities first.

Addressing vulnerabilities typically involves a series of steps. Remediation efforts aim to patch, mitigate, or fix the vulnerabilities identified. Monitoring systems and networks continuously helps detect any new vulnerabilities that may emerge over time. Documentation of vulnerability assessments and remediation efforts is crucial, providing an audit trail, supporting compliance, and tracking progress. Education and training programs promote a culture of security awareness within an organization, helping individuals recognize and report potential security weaknesses. Finally, an incident response plan is essential to contain and recover from incidents if vulnerabilities are exploited.

However, the identification of vulnerabilities is not without its challenges. Factors like the scale of IT environments, the evolving threat landscape, false positives from automated tools, resource constraints, privacy and compliance considerations, and third-party dependencies contribute to the complexity of vulnerability assessment.

In conclusion, identifying vulnerabilities is not merely a cybersecurity best practice; it is an imperative in the digital age. It is the foundation upon which effective cybersecurity strategies are built. While the methodologies and techniques used for vulnerability assessment are diverse and continually evolving, the subsequent actions taken—remediation, monitoring, documentation, education, and incident response—are what truly strengthen an organization's security posture. In an interconnected and ever-changing digital world, the quest to identify and address vulnerabilities remains a perpetual and essential endeavor. It is a testament to the ongoing commitment to safeguarding against the relentless tide of cyber threats.

Real-world examples of cyberattacks

In the digital age, where our lives and livelihoods are increasingly dependent on technology, the specter of cyberattacks looms large. These attacks, often perpetrated by malicious actors seeking financial gain, political advantage, or simply chaos, can have far- reaching and devastating consequences. Real-world examples of cyberattacks serve as stark reminders of the vulnerabilities that exist in our interconnected world. In this section, we will explore some notable cyberattacks, ranging from massive data breaches to disruptive ransomware attacks and state-sponsored cyber espionage. These incidents provide valuable insights into the evolving landscape of cyber threats and the urgent need for robust cybersecurity measures.

In 2017, Equifax, one of the three major credit-reporting companies in the United States, fell victim to a colossal data breach. The breach exposed the personal information of approximately 147 million individuals, making it one of the largest and most impactful data breaches in history. Hackers obtained unauthorized access to confidential information by taking advantage of a vulnerability in the website software of the business.

The Equifax breach underscored the critical importance of data security and the consequences of failing to protect sensitive information adequately. Social security numbers, names, addresses, and other personal data were exposed, putting individuals at risk of identity theft and financial fraud. This incident prompted widespread public concern, congressional inquiries, and legal actions against the company.

In May 2017, the world witnessed the rapid spread of the WannaCry ransomware, which affected over 150 country's hundreds of thousands of computers. The ransomware encrypted files on infected systems and demanded a ransom in Bitcoin for the decryption key. The attack affected critical infrastructure, including healthcare systems in the United Kingdom, leading to the cancellation of medical procedures and patient data being held hostage.

WannaCry served as a global wake-up call to the potential impact of ransomware attacks on essential services. It highlighted the vulnerability of outdated and unpatched systems to cyber threats. The ransomware exploited a known Windows vulnerability, for which Microsoft had released a security patch months earlier. The event made clear how important it is to update software and put strong cybersecurity procedures in place in order to guard against ransomware and other malware.

The NotPetya ransomware attack, which struck in June 2017, initially appeared to be a ransomware campaign similar to WannaCry. However, as investigations unfolded, it became clear that NotPetya was more insidious. It was not designed to collect ransoms but to cause widespread disruption and destruction.

NotPetya primarily targeted Ukrainian organizations but quickly spread beyond Ukraine's borders, affecting numerous multinational companies. It exploited a compromised software update mechanism, allowing it to infiltrate systems. Once inside, it encrypted files and overwrote the master boot record, rendering infected computers inoperable.

This attack had a lasting impact on organizations, revealing the potential for state-sponsored cyberattacks to disrupt global business operations. NotPetya is widely believed to have been the work of Russian state actors, further highlighting the blurred lines between cybercriminals and nation-states in the world of cyber warfare.

In late 2020, the SolarWinds supply chain attack came to light, exposing a new level of sophistication in cyber espionage. This highly covert operation targeted SolarWinds, a major software vendor whose products are widely used for network monitoring and management. The attackers compromised SolarWinds' software build process, injecting a malicious backdoor into software updates.

This backdoor, known as Sunburst or Solorigate, was distributed to SolarWinds' customers, including numerous government agencies and Fortune 500 companies. Once installed, it allowed the attackers to infiltrate networks, exfiltrate sensitive data, and conduct espionage activities for months without detection.

The SolarWinds incident revealed the formidable capabilities of nation-state actors in carrying out long-term, stealthy cyber espionage operations. It raised questions about the security of software supply chains and the need for enhanced security measures to prevent such attacks.

In May 2021, the Colonial Pipeline, which supplies nearly half of the fuel consumed on the U.S. East Coast, fell victim to a ransomware attack carried out by the DarkSide ransomware group. The attack forced the company to shut down its pipeline operations, causing fuel shortages and panic buying in several states.

The Colonial Pipeline attack highlighted the critical role of critical infrastructure in modern society and the potential consequences of cyberattacks on essential services. It also raised questions about the ethics of paying ransoms to cybercriminals, as Colonial Pipeline reportedly paid a multi-million-dollar ransom to regain access to its systems.

Real-world examples of cyberattacks serve as harsh reminders of the vulnerabilities that exist in our interconnected digital world. They serve as valuable lessons for individuals, organizations, and governments alike, highlighting the urgent need for robust cybersecurity measures, proactive defenses, and a collective commitment to safeguarding against cyber threats. The evolving landscape of cyber threats demands continuous adaptation and resilience to ensure the security and integrity of our digital infrastructure.

CHAPTER V

The Hacking Methodology

Steps in the hacking process (Reconnaissance, scanning, exploitation, etc.)

In the realm of cybersecurity, knowledge is power. Understanding the steps malicious hackers follow to infiltrate systems and compromise data is a fundamental defense component. The hacking process, often depicted as a series of stages, encompasses reconnaissance, scanning, exploitation, privilege escalation, maintaining access, and covering tracks. Each step serves a distinct purpose in the cyber intruder's quest for unauthorized access and control. In this section, we will delve into these steps, shedding light on the techniques and tactics employed by hackers and the countermeasures organizations can adopt to thwart their efforts.

The hacking process typically begins with reconnaissance, where hackers gather information about their target. This phase can involve passive and active reconnaissance. Passive reconnaissance entails collecting data without directly engaging with the target, such as through open-source research, social media analysis, or publicly available information. On the other hand, active reconnaissance involves probing the target's systems to discover vulnerabilities or weaknesses. Techniques like port scanning, DNS enumeration, and network mapping fall under this category. The information collected during reconnaissance is crucial for hackers to craft their attack strategy effectively.

Once hackers have a clear picture of their target, they move on to scanning, where they actively seek vulnerabilities in the target's systems. Port scanning is a common scanning technique used to identify open ports and services that may be potential entry points. Vulnerability scanning involves searching for known weaknesses or misconfigurations in software, operating systems, or network devices. Scanning tools like Nmap and Nessus are commonly employed in this phase. The goal of scanning is to identify points of entry for exploitation.

Exploitation is the critical phase where hackers leverage the vulnerabilities discovered during scanning to gain unauthorized access to the target system or network. This may involve exploiting software vulnerabilities, weak passwords, or misconfigured security settings. Common exploitation techniques include buffer overflow attacks, SQL injection, and the use of malware or exploits to compromise target systems. Once access is achieved, hackers may establish a foothold, often in the form of a backdoor or remote access tool, to maintain control and persistence within the target environment.

After gaining initial access, hackers often seek to escalate their privileges within the target system or network. Privilege escalation involves obtaining higher-level access rights or administrative privileges, which provide more extensive control and access to critical resources. This step can be achieved by exploiting additional vulnerabilities, leveraging weak access controls, or using privilege escalation exploits. Once hackers acquire elevated privileges, they can access and manipulate sensitive data and system configurations.

Maintaining access is critical for hackers to ensure their continued presence within the target environment. They employ various tactics to maintain persistence, including installing rootkits, Trojans, or other forms of malware that allow them to retain control over compromised systems. Backdoors and command-and-control (C2) servers are often used to establish covert communication channels with compromised systems, enabling hackers to receive instructions, exfiltrate data, and launch further attacks.

Hackers cover tracks, the final phase of the hacking process to evade detection and minimize the risk of discovery. This involves erasing digital footprints and removing evidence of their activities from compromised systems and logs. Hackers may alter or delete log files, modify system timestamps, and remove any traces of their presence, making it challenging for security professionals to trace their actions. This step is critical for maintaining stealth and operational security.

Understanding the steps in the hacking process is invaluable for organizations looking to defend against cyber threats. Robust cybersecurity practices and countermeasures can mitigate the risks associated with each phase.

The hacking process, consisting of reconnaissance, scanning, exploitation, privilege escalation, maintaining access, and covering tracks, serves as a blueprint for cyber intruders seeking unauthorized access and control. Understanding these phases is essential for organizations and cybersecurity professionals to develop effective defense strategies and countermeasures. The cybersecurity cat-and-mouse game continues in a constantly evolving threat landscape, with defenders striving to stay one step ahead of determined adversaries.

By leveraging knowledge of the hacking process and implementing proactive cybersecurity measures, organizations can enhance their resilience against cyber threats and safeguard their digital assets.

Tools and techniques used by ethical hackers

In an increasingly interconnected world, the importance of cybersecurity has never been more evident. With the rapid expansion of digital infrastructure, protecting sensitive data, critical systems, and personal information has become a paramount concern. Ethical hackers, also known as white-hat hackers or security researchers, play a pivotal role in safeguarding this digital realm. They harness their skills, knowledge, and many tools and techniques to proactively identify vulnerabilities and weaknesses in systems, networks, and applications. In this section, we will explore the world of ethical hacking, shedding light on the tools and techniques employed by these guardians of the digital realm.

Ethical hacking deliberately and legally probes computer systems, networks, and applications to uncover vulnerabilities and weaknesses. The primary goal of ethical hackers is to identify security flaws before malicious hackers can exploit them, thereby helping organizations fortify their defenses. Ethical hackers typically work with the full consent and cooperation of the system's owner and follow strict ethical guidelines during their assessments.

To evaluate the security posture of their targets, ethical hackers use a wide variety of tools and methods. These resources and methods fall into a few general categories:

Ethical hackers start their assessments with network scanning and enumeration. The goal is to gather information about the target network's structure, identify active hosts, and discover potential vulnerabilities. Tools like Nmap, Wireshark, and Netcat are indispensable in this phase. Nmap, short for Network Mapper, is a versatile open-source tool employed for network discovery and security auditing. It can scan and map networks, discover open ports, identify running services, and provide information about the target network's topology. Wireshark, a network packet analyzer, allows ethical hackers to capture and analyze network traffic, which is invaluable for inspecting packets, diagnosing network issues, and identifying potential security vulnerabilities. Netcat, often called the "Swiss Army knife" of networking, is a versatile command-line utility. Ethical hackers use it for port scanning, banner grabbing, and establishing reverse shells for remote access.

After identifying potential entry points through network scanning, ethical hackers move on to vulnerability scanning and assessment. This phase involves actively searching for known vulnerabilities, misconfigurations, and security weaknesses in systems and networks. Tools such as Nessus, OpenVAS, and Qualys are essential in this context. Nessus is a popular vulnerability scanner that automates the process of determining security weaknesses in systems and networks. It provides detailed reports on discovered vulnerabilities, their severity, and suggested remediation steps. OpenVAS (Open Vulnerability Assessment System), an open-source alternative to Nessus, offers similar capabilities, allowing ethical hackers to scan for vulnerabilities, misconfigurations, and potential security risks. Qualys, a cloud-based vulnerability management platform, provides scanning, assessment, and reporting services, helping organizations identify and remediate vulnerabilities proactively.

In the digital age, web applications are prevalent and frequently targeted by malicious hackers. Ethical hackers use specialized tools to assess the security of web applications, searching for vulnerabilities that could be exploited. Burp Suite and OWASP ZAP are among this category's most widely used tools. Burp Suite is a potent web application security testing tool. It is widely used for web vulnerability scanning, proxying, and web application security analysis. An open-source web application security scanner is called OWASP ZAP, short for the OWASP Zed Attack Proxy. It helps ethical hackers find security vulnerabilities in web applications, including cross-site scripting (XSS) and SQL injection.

Strong authentication mechanisms are critical for securing systems and networks. Ethical hackers use password cracking tools to test the strength of passwords and authentication mechanisms. John the Ripper and Hydra are two popular tools in this category. John the Ripper is a widely utilized password cracking tool that can crack different password hashes using various attack methods, including dictionary attacks and brute force. Hydra is a versatile password-cracking tool that supports numerous protocols, including HTTP, SSH, and FTP. It tests the strength of authentication mechanisms by attempting to guess passwords.

Once vulnerabilities have been identified, ethical hackers may attempt to utilize them to gain unauthorized access to systems or networks. Tools like Metasploit and PowerShell are commonly used in this phase. Metasploit is a penetration testing framework that provides tools for exploiting known vulnerabilities. It also offers a wide range of post-exploitation modules for maintaining access and control on compromised systems. PowerShell, a scripting language and framework developed by Microsoft, is a versatile tool that ethical hackers use for various purposes, including running scripts to exploit vulnerabilities and conduct post-exploitation activities.

Wireless networks are prevalent in both home and corporate environments, making them attractive targets for attackers. Ethical hackers use specialized tools to assess the security of wireless networks. Aircrack-ng is a suite of tools commonly employed for this purpose. Aircrack-ng can be used to crack WEP and WPA/WPA2-PSK encryption keys, conduct packet sniffing, and perform other wireless attacks.

Social engineering attacks manipulate human psychology to deceive individuals into revealing confidential information or taking specific actions. Ethical hackers use tools like the Social-Engineer Toolkit (SET) to simulate and test social engineering attacks. SET is a collection of social engineering tools that ethical hackers use to craft convincing phishing emails, clone websites, and simulate social engineering attacks.

In the aftermath of a security incident, it is essential to conduct digital forensics to gather evidence, understand the scope of the breach, and identify the attackers. Autopsy is an open-source digital forensics platform used for analyzing disk images and performing forensic investigations. Ethical hackers use Autopsy and similar tools to examine evidence and gather information forensically soundly.

Ethical hackers are on the frontlines of cybersecurity, tirelessly working to identify and mitigate vulnerabilities before malicious hackers can exploit them. Their expertise, combined with the extensive toolbox of tools and techniques at their disposal, empowers organizations to bolster their defenses and protect sensitive data and critical systems. As technology advances and cyber threats evolve, ethical hacking remains an essential and dynamic field, dedicated to ensuring the security and integrity of the digital realm. Ethical hackers stand as champions of a safer, more secure digital future in the ongoing battle between cybersecurity professionals and cybercriminals.

Hands-on exercises and demonstrations

In a world that is becoming increasingly digital, cybersecurity has become a top priority for people, businesses, and governments. With the ever-evolving landscape of cyber threats, organizations need skilled professionals who can identify vulnerabilities, protect against attacks, and safeguard critical digital assets. Ethical hackers, also known as white-hat hackers, play a crucial role in this endeavor. They are cybersecurity experts who actively probe systems, networks, and applications to uncover vulnerabilities before malicious hackers can exploit them. To excel in this field, ethical hackers require theoretical knowledge and practical skills honed through hands-on exercises and demonstrations. This section explores the significance of practical training for ethical hackers, delves into the critical components of such training, and discusses its broader implications for the cybersecurity landscape.

Its dynamic and evolving nature marks the realm of cybersecurity. New vulnerabilities and attack vectors emerge regularly, while cybercriminals continuously adapt their tactics. To stay ahead of these threats, ethical hackers must equip themselves with practical skills that enable them to identify, assess, and mitigate security risks effectively. While theoretical knowledge provides a foundational understanding of cybersecurity principles, hands-on exercises and demonstrations bridge the gap between theory and practice, allowing ethical hackers to gain real-world experience and problem-solving abilities.

Practical training for ethical hackers comprises various components that together create a comprehensive and immersive learning experience:

Hands-on exercises often occur in controlled laboratory environments, commonly called "labs." These labs replicate real-world network and system configurations, allowing ethical hackers to experiment without the risk of compromising live systems. Labs can be physical, comprising actual hardware and network setups, or virtual, where environments are emulated using software and virtualization technologies.

Practical training involves simulated attacks and scenarios that mimic the techniques employed by malicious hackers. These exercises expose ethical hackers to various attack vectors, such as network exploitation, web application vulnerabilities, social engineering, and wireless attacks. By immersing themselves in these scenarios, ethical hackers gain valuable insights into attacker methodologies and vulnerabilities that may exist in different environments.

The use of ethical hacking tools and technologies is a fundamental aspect of hands-on training. Ethical hackers become proficient in using scanning tools, vulnerability assessment tools, penetration testing frameworks like Metasploit, and other specialized software designed for security assessments. Mastery of these tools is essential for conducting effective evaluations and identifying vulnerabilities.

Capture the Flag challenges are interactive and competitive exercises in which ethical hackers solve puzzles and complete tasks to obtain flags or tokens. These challenges encompass various cybersecurity domains, including cryptography, reverse engineering, forensics, and network exploitation. CTF challenges promote problem-solving, critical thinking, and collaboration among participants, making them a valuable hands-on training component.

Ethical hackers engage in exercises that exploit vulnerabilities they discover during their assessments. This includes gaining unauthorized access to systems, escalating privileges, and maintaining persistence. Vulnerability assessment exercises focus on identifying and evaluating vulnerabilities in systems, networks, and applications, enabling ethical hackers to provide detailed recommendations for remediation.

Incident response simulations place ethical hackers in scenarios where they must respond to security incidents promptly. These exercises may involve investigating suspected breaches, analyzing malware, containing and mitigating the impact of security incidents, and developing incident response plans. Incident response simulations prepare ethical hackers to handle real-world incidents effectively and minimize potential damage.

Hands-on exercises and demonstrations offer several significant benefits to ethical hackers:

The practical nature of hands-on training enhances the skills and expertise of ethical hackers. They learn to navigate real-world challenges, make informed decisions under pressure, and develop a deep understanding of security vulnerabilities and attack vectors.

Practical training often presents ethical hackers with complex and novel challenges. These exercises encourage them to think critically, adjust to shifting circumstances, and come up with creative solutions to security problems.

Hands-on exercises provide a taste of what it's like to work as an ethical hacker in the field. This experience is invaluable for those seeking to transition into cybersecurity roles, as it bridges the gap between theory and practical application.

Ethical hackers with rigorous practical training are better equipped to help organizations defend against cyber threats. They can identify vulnerabilities that may elude automated scanners and develop custom mitigation strategies tailored to specific environments.

Hands-on training often involves teamwork and collaboration among participants. Ethical hackers learn to communicate effectively, share knowledge, and work together to solve complex challenges. These skills are essential in the field, where collaboration between security professionals is common, especially in response to sophisticated attacks.

While hands-on exercises and demonstrations are indispensable in ethical hacking training, they come with their set of challenges:

Setting up and maintaining realistic laboratory environments can be resource-intensive. Organizations and training providers must invest in hardware, software, and infrastructure to support hands-on training adequately. This can be a barrier to entry for individuals and smaller organizations.

Practical exercises can inadvertently expose sensitive data or systems to unintended risks. Hackers must operate within strict ethical boundaries to ensure their activities do not compromise security or privacy. Confidential information must be handled with care, and exercises should be conducted in a controlled environment.

Participants in hands-on training programs often have varying levels of expertise, ranging from beginners to experienced professionals. Instructors must tailor exercises to accommodate participants with different skill levels while ensuring that advanced learners are adequately challenged.

Access to quality hands-on training can be costly, limiting opportunities for some individuals, particularly those with limited financial resources. Ensuring accessibility to training resources and labs is an ongoing challenge within the cybersecurity community.

As the cybersecurity landscape evolves, the role of ethical hackers in protecting digital assets becomes increasingly critical. Hands-on exercises and demonstrations will remain at the forefront of ethical hacking training, evolving to address emerging threats and technologies. Moreover, integrating gamification, artificial intelligence, and virtual reality into training platforms promises to make practical training even more engaging and effective.

These innovations will further enhance the realism and effectiveness of hands-on training, providing ethical hackers with the skills to counter evolving cyber threats effectively.

Hands-on exercises and demonstrations are the bedrock of ethical hacking training. They provide aspiring ethical hackers with the practical skills and experience necessary to excel in the field of cybersecurity. By immersing themselves in realistic scenarios, ethical hackers learn to think like attackers, identify vulnerabilities, and develop effective strategies for securing systems and networks. As the demand for skilled cybersecurity professionals continues to rise, hands-on training will remain essential in building a capable and agile workforce dedicated to defending against cyber threats. In the ever-evolving battle between ethical hackers and malicious actors, practical expertise gained through hands-on training is a powerful weapon to safeguard the digital realm.

CHAPTER VI

Penetration Testing

Understanding penetration testing

In the ever-evolving landscape of cybersecurity, one practice stands out as a critical component of safeguarding digital assets and data: penetration testing. Often referred to as pen testing, this methodological and controlled approach to hacking is a proactive effort to identify vulnerabilities in computer systems, networks, and applications before malicious actors can exploit them. Penetration testing is not about breaching security for nefarious purposes; it is a valuable tool for strengthening defenses, assessing risk, and ensuring that organizations are well-prepared to withstand cyber threats.

At its core, penetration testing is akin to a digital safety drill. It simulates real-world cyberattacks to assess an organization's vulnerabilities and defenses. Ethical hackers, often employed as penetration testers, assume the role of adversaries to identify weaknesses that malicious actors could exploit. This process provides organizations with an invaluable opportunity to uncover security flaws, assess the potential impact of a breach, and take corrective action before a real threat materializes.

Penetration testing typically follows a structured process that can be broken down into numerous key phases. While the exact methodology may vary depending on the objectives and scope of the test, a common approach includes the following stages:

Planning and Scoping: The first step involves defining the scope of the penetration test, which include the systems, networks, as well as the applications to be tested. Goals, objectives, and rules of engagement are established, ensuring that all participants clearly understand the testing parameters.

Reconnaissance: This phase mimics the initial information-gathering stage that a malicious hacker would undertake. Ethical hackers collect data about the target environment, including IP addresses, domain names, and potential entry points.

Scanning: Armed with reconnaissance data, the penetration tester scans the target systems and networks for vulnerabilities. This may involve network scanning to identify open ports, services, and potential weak points.

Enumeration: In this stage, the tester delves deeper to gather specific information about the target systems. This may include identifying user accounts, services, and configurations.

Exploitation: Once vulnerabilities are identified, the penetration tester attempts to exploit them to acquire unauthorized access or control. Successful exploitation demonstrates the potential impact of a real-world cyberattack.

Maintaining Access: In some cases, maintaining access to the compromised system is crucial for further analysis. This phase mimics the actions of an attacker who seeks to maintain control over the compromised system.

Covering Tracks: Ethical hackers often leave traces of their activities during testing. In this phase, they attempt to erase any evidence of their presence to mimic the actions of a real attacker.

Reporting: Following the penetration test, a comprehensive report is prepared. This report details the vulnerabilities discovered, the potential impact of exploitation, and recommendations for remediation. It serves as a roadmap for strengthening security.

Penetration tests can take various forms, depending on the specific objectives and the testers' level of knowledge about the target environment. Three common types of penetration tests are:

Black-Box Testing: The penetration tester is blind to the target environment during a black-box test. This simulates an external attacker with limited information attempting to breach the system.

White-Box Testing: White-box testing, on the other hand, provides the penetration tester with detailed information about the target environment. This can include network diagrams, system configurations, and source code. It simulates an insider threat or a highly informed external attacker.

Grey-Box Testing: Grey-box testing strikes a balance between black-box and white-box approaches. Testers have partial knowledge of the target environment, mimicking a scenario where an attacker may have obtained some insider information.

Penetration testing offers a multitude of benefits for organizations. It identifies vulnerabilities before malicious actors can exploit them, assesses the real-world impact of security flaws, and aids in compliance with industry regulations. It also improves incident response and enhances overall security awareness within the organization. However, it is crucial to approach penetration testing with care, ensuring that ethical hackers follow strict rules of engagement and confidentiality.

In conclusion, penetration testing is a cornerstone of modern cybersecurity practices. It serves as a proactive defense mechanism against cyber threats, allowing organizations to identify and remediate vulnerabilities before they are exploited. Through a structured and controlled approach, ethical hackers uncover weaknesses, assess risks, and provide recommendations for strengthening defenses. In an era where data breaches and cyberattacks are constant threats, penetration testing represents a crucial line of defense in the ongoing battle to safeguard digital assets and data.

Types of penetration tests (black-box, white-box, grey-box)

In the ever-evolving cybersecurity landscape, where threats lurk around every digital corner, organizations must employ a proactive and comprehensive approach to safeguard their data and systems. One of the fundamental strategies in this ongoing battle is penetration testing, a systematic process of identifying security weaknesses before malicious actors can exploit them. Penetration tests come in various forms, each tailored to specific objectives and levels of information about the target systems. This section explores the three primary types of penetration tests: black-box testing, white-box testing, and grey-box testing. By understanding these approaches, organizations can better determine which type of penetration test suits their needs and contributes most effectively to their overall cybersecurity posture.

Black-box testing, often referred to as external testing or blind testing, simulates the perspective of an uninformed attacker who possesses minimal to no knowledge of the target system. This approach provides the penetration tester with limited or no prior information about the organization's infrastructure, network architecture, or internal workings. The objective is to emulate a real-world scenario where an external hacker attempts to breach the organization's defenses without any insider information.

The black-box tester begins with reconnaissance activities, gathering publicly available information through techniques like open-source intelligence (OSINT) research, domain name system (DNS) enumeration, and social engineering assessments. These initial steps help the tester gain insights into the organization's online presence, employee information, and potential entry points. Armed with this limited information, the tester scans and enumerates the target systems, identifies open ports and services, and searches for vulnerabilities.

The primary advantage of black-box testing lies in its realism. It provides an accurate representation of how external attackers might approach a target. However, it can also present challenges, as the lack of internal knowledge may result in certain vulnerabilities being overlooked, especially if they are deeply embedded within the system.

In stark contrast to black-box testing, white-box testing, also known as clear box testing, adopts the perspective of an insider with full knowledge of the target system. This approach provides the penetration tester with complete information about the organization's network architecture, system configurations, source code, and other internal details.

White-box testing typically involves close collaboration between the organization's IT or security team and the penetration tester. The tester gains access to detailed documentation, network diagrams, system credentials, and, in some cases, the actual source code of applications. Armed with this comprehensive understanding, the white-box tester can conduct an in-depth analysis of the system's vulnerabilities.

The advantages of white-box testing are evident. Testers can thoroughly assess the target system's security, identifying vulnerabilities that may be challenging to discover in other approaches. This level of transparency enables organizations to address vulnerabilities at a granular level, making it particularly valuable for mission-critical systems and applications.

However, white-box testing does have its limitations. It may not fully replicate the mindset and actions of an external attacker who lacks insider knowledge. Additionally, the tester's familiarity with the system could lead to biases or assumptions that an external attacker would not have.

Grey-box testing strikes a balance between the black-box and white-box approaches, offering the advantages of both while mitigating some of their drawbacks. In grey-box testing, the penetration tester possesses partial knowledge of the target environment. This limited insider information may include high-level network diagrams, system architecture overviews, or general knowledge about the organization's infrastructure.

The grey-box tester conducts assessments with this intermediate level of understanding, simulating an attacker with limited insider information. This approach enable for a more realistic assessment than pure white-box testing while still providing some insights that black-box testing lacks. The tester begins with reconnaissance and scanning activities, much like in black-box testing, but with the added benefit of context from partial knowledge.

Grey-box testing is often considered a pragmatic compromise, balancing realism and insight. It is beneficial when organizations seek a comprehensive assessment but do not want to provide full access to internal systems. Grey-box testing can identify vulnerabilities that are more challenging to discover in purely black-box reviews while maintaining a degree of realism.

The choice of penetration test type depends on various factors, including an organization's objectives, resources, and the specific systems or applications under assessment. Each type has its strengths and weaknesses, making it essential to consider the following factors when making a selection:

Organizations should define their objectives clearly. Are they primarily concerned with simulating external threats? Or do they need a deep dive into the security of their internal systems and applications? Understanding the goals of the assessment guides the choice of the appropriate type.

The resources available for the penetration test play a crucial role. White-box testing, which requires collaboration and access to internal systems, demands more resources in terms of time and personnel. Conversely, black-box testing may be more resource-efficient but could overlook specific vulnerabilities.

Consider the level of realism desired in the assessment. Black-box testing provides a realistic external perspective, while white-box testing offers an insider's view. Grey-box testing balances these extremes, offering a compromise between realism and insight.

Organizations must assess their risk tolerance. A white-box assessment may be necessary for highly sensitive systems or applications to uncover all potential vulnerabilities. However, a black-box or grey-box approach may suffice for less critical systems.

Regulatory requirements and industry standards may dictate the type of penetration testing required. Some regulations explicitly specify the need for white-box assessments for specific critical systems or data.

The complexity of the target systems and applications can influence the choice of penetration test type. Highly complex systems may benefit from a white-box assessment to ensure a thorough examination.

Penetration testing is vital to a robust cybersecurity strategy, allowing organizations to identify and remediate vulnerabilities proactively. The choice of penetration test type—black-box, white-box, or grey-box—depends on many factors, including objectives, resources, realism, risk tolerance, regulatory compliance, and system complexity. By comprehending the strengths and weaknesses of each approach, organizations can make informed decisions that align with their specific needs and contribute to a more resilient cybersecurity posture. Ultimately, the goal is to uncover vulnerabilities from different angles and fortify defenses against the ever-evolving landscape of cyber threats.

Conducting a penetration test

In the relentless struggle to protect valuable digital assets from an ever-evolving landscape of cyber threats, organizations employ various cybersecurity measures. Among these strategies, penetration testing is a formidable tool, enabling organizations to identify and mitigate vulnerabilities in their systems and networks proactively. This section delves into the intricacies of conducting a penetration test, a meticulous process that mirrors the actions of potential attackers while adhering to ethical guidelines. From the first planning steps to the final reporting and remediation, every facet of the penetration testing journey is a critical step toward fortifying an organization's cybersecurity defenses.

Before embarking on a penetration test, it is essential to describe the scope and objectives of the assessment. The basis for the entire testing procedure is laid during this first stage. The scope outlines the boundaries of the test, specifying the systems, applications, and network segments to be assessed. It determines whether the test will be conducted internally (within the organization's network) or externally (from an external perspective). It also identifies constraints, such as time limitations or specific compliance requirements.

Simultaneously, the objectives of the penetration test must be clearly articulated. These objectives often align with the organization's overarching security goals and may include identifying critical vulnerabilities, evaluating the effectiveness of security controls, or assessing incident response procedures. Establishing well-defined objectives ensures that the test remains focused and delivers actionable results.

With the scope and objectives established, the penetration testing journey begins with reconnaissance. This phase mimics the actions of a potential attacker gathering information about the target environment. Reconnaissance encompasses both passive and active techniques to build a comprehensive picture of the organization's digital footprint.

Passive reconnaissance involves the collection of publicly available information. Open-source intelligence (OSINT) research is a fundamental component, wherein testers scour publicly accessible sources, including websites, social media, and public records, to glean information about the organization. This may include details about employees, job roles, email addresses, and technology stack.

On the other hand, active reconnaissance involves more direct interactions with the target. This may include domain name system (DNS) enumeration, which seeks to identify subdomains associated with the organization. Additionally, testers may engage in social engineering assessments, attempting to manipulate individuals within the organization to divulge sensitive information.

Following reconnaissance, penetration testers move on to scanning and enumeration. These activities are akin to probing the outer defenses of a fortress, seeking vulnerabilities that could potentially be exploited. Scanning involves using various tools and techniques to discover open network ports and services on target systems. Testers may employ port scanning to identify these open entry points.

Enumeration takes scanning a step further, seeking to extract detailed information about systems, users, and network resources. This phase aims to uncover valuable insights that could lead to potential vulnerabilities. Enumeration may include querying network services for information, extracting user lists, and mapping network topologies.

The results of scanning and enumeration provide a roadmap for subsequent phases of the penetration test. Vulnerabilities identified during this stage are critical targets for further assessment.

With a wealth of information gathered from reconnaissance, scanning, and enumeration, penetration testers enter the vulnerability assessment phase. This is where the meticulous process of evaluating potential vulnerabilities begins. Testers analyze the results of scanning and enumeration to pinpoint security weaknesses.

The assessment encompasses many vulnerabilities, including known software vulnerabilities, misconfigurations, and security weaknesses specific to the organization's environment. Vulnerabilities are categorized based on their severity, potential impact, and ease of exploitation. This prioritization helps organizations focus their efforts on addressing the most critical issues first.

During the vulnerability assessment, penetration testers may utilize specialized tools and techniques to identify vulnerabilities. This includes vulnerability scanning tools that automate the process of identifying known vulnerabilities in software and systems.

Once vulnerabilities are identified during the assessment phase, the penetration testers proceed to exploitation. This is the heart of the penetration test, where testers simulate real-world attacks to determine the feasibility of unauthorized access and assess the potential damage that an attacker could inflict.

Successful exploitation may involve controlling systems, escalating privileges, and exfiltrating sensitive data. It is crucial to note that exploitation is conducted within the confines of ethical hacking guidelines, ensuring that the actions taken do not result in actual harm or disruption to the organization's operations.

Exploitation techniques can vary widely, depending on the specific vulnerabilities and systems being assessed. Testers may use custom scripts, known exploits, or sophisticated attack vectors to compromise target systems.

Following successful exploitation, penetration testers delve into post-exploitation activities. This phase is critical for evaluating the effectiveness of an organization's security controls in detecting and responding to intrusions.

Post-exploitation activities may include maintaining access to compromised systems to assess how long an attacker could persist undetected. Testers may also conduct lateral movement within the network, attempting to pivot from compromised systems to more critical assets. Additionally, covering digital tracks and erasing any evidence of the intrusion is a key aspect of post-exploitation activities.

The insights gained during post-exploitation help organizations enhance their incident response procedures. Organizations must be prepared to find and respond to real-world breaches effectively.

The culmination of the penetration test is the reporting and remediation phase. This is where the test results are synthesized into a comprehensive report that details the vulnerabilities discovered, their potential impact, and recommended steps for remediation.

The penetration test report serves as a valuable resource for organizations to prioritize and address security weaknesses. It entails actionable insights that allow organizations to strengthen their security posture. The report typically includes an executive summary for high-level stakeholders and technical details for IT and security teams.

Upon receiving the report, organizations initiate the remediation process. This involves taking steps to mitigate or eliminate the identified vulnerabilities. Remediation efforts may include patching software, reconfiguring systems, and enhancing security controls. The goal is to bolster the organization's defenses against potential threats based on the penetration test findings.

Conducting a penetration test is not a one-time event but rather part of an ongoing cybersecurity strategy. Threats evolve, and systems change, necessitating regular assessments to ensure that vulnerabilities are continuously identified and addressed.

The results of penetration tests feed into the organization's security improvement cycle, helping to refine security policies, enhance incident response procedures, and fine-tune security controls. Additionally, organizations can use the insights gained from penetration tests to prioritize future investments in cybersecurity measures.

Conducting a penetration test is a multifaceted journey that emulates the actions of potential attackers while adhering to ethical guidelines. It starts with defining the scope and objectives, proceeds through reconnaissance, scanning, enumeration, vulnerability assessment, exploitation, post-exploitation, and culminates in reporting and remediation. Each phase is critical in uncovering vulnerabilities and providing actionable insights for organizations to strengthen their cybersecurity defenses.

By embracing penetration testing as an integral component of their cybersecurity strategy, organizations proactively identify and mitigate vulnerabilities before malicious actors can exploit them. In an era marked by relentless cyber threats, the penetration test serves as a vital tool in the ongoing battle to protect digital assets and ensure the resilience of organizations in the face of evolving security challenges.

CHAPTER VII

Protecting Your Systems

Cybersecurity best practices

In an increasingly digitized world where information flows freely across networks and technology underpins nearly every aspect of modern life, the importance of cybersecurity cannot be overstated. The proliferation of cyber threats and the potential consequences of security breaches have elevated the significance of adopting robust cybersecurity practices. This section explores a comprehensive set of cybersecurity best practices that individuals and organizations can implement to protect their digital assets and shield against a wide array of cyber threats. From proactive measures such as employee training and robust access controls to defensive strategies like encryption and incident response planning, these practices serve as a foundational framework for bolstering cybersecurity defenses.

A cornerstone of cybersecurity best practices is fostering an organization's security culture. This begins with employee training and awareness programs. Human error remains to be one of the leading causes of security incidents, and educating employees about the risks and best practices is essential. Training should cover subjects like recognizing phishing emails, creating strong passwords, and identifying social engineering tactics. Regular awareness campaigns and simulated phishing exercises can reinforce these lessons and help employees stay vigilant.

Access control is a fundamental element of cybersecurity. Strong access controls ensure that only authorized individuals can access sensitive data and systems. This involves using robust authentication methods such as multi-factor authentication (or MFA) and enforcing the principle of least privilege (or PoLP), which grants users the minimum access necessary to perform their roles. Regularly reviewing and updating access permissions is also crucial to prevent unauthorized access.

Outdated software and unpatched vulnerabilities are common targets for cyberattacks. Cybercriminals exploit known weaknesses to gain access to systems and data. To mitigate this risk, organizations should establish a robust patch management process that regularly applies security updates and patches to all software and systems. Automated tools can assist streamline this process and ensure that critical vulnerabilities are addressed promptly.

Network security is paramount to protect against a range of threats. Implementing firewalls, intrusion detection systems (IDS), and intrusion prevention systems (IPS) can help safeguard network traffic and detect suspicious activities. Network segmentation is another best practice, isolating critical assets from less secure parts of the network to limit the potential influence of a breach.

Encrypting sensitive data at rest as well as in transit is crucial to protect against data breaches. Encryption guarantees that even if data is compromised, it remains unreadable without the appropriate decryption key. This practice is essential for data stored in the cloud and data transmitted over public networks.

Passwords serve as the first line of defense for many systems and accounts. Implementing secure password practices, such as using complex, unique passwords for every account, changing passwords regularly, and storing them securely, can significantly reduce the risk of unauthorized access. Password managers can assist individuals in generating and managing strong, unique passwords.

No organization is immune to security incidents. A well-defined incident response plan is vital to minimize the impact of an incident and facilitate a swift recovery. The plan should outline the steps to take in the event of a breach, including incident detection, containment, investigation, communication, and recovery efforts. Regularly testing and updating the plan ensures it remains effective.

Proactively monitoring networks and also systems for signs of malicious activity is crucial to detecting threats early. SIEM, often called Security information and event management solutions can help organizations collect and analyze security-related data, providing insights into potential threats. Real-time monitoring allows for immediate response to suspicious activities.

The mobile devices proliferation in the workplace introduces new security challenges. Implementing mobile device management (MDM) solutions allows organizations to enforce security policies on mobile devices like smartphones and tablets. This includes features like remote device wipe, encryption, and app whitelisting.

Regularly assessing an organization's security posture through audits and assessments helps identify vulnerabilities and weaknesses. These assessments can include penetration testing, vulnerability scanning, and security audits. The results inform security improvements and ensure compliance with industry regulations and standards.

Establishing security into the software development lifecycle is crucial to avoid introducing vulnerabilities during the development process. Secure coding practices, code reviews, and application security testing are essential to identify and remediate security issues in software applications.

Third-party vendors and suppliers can introduce security risks into an organization. Establishing a robust vendor risk management program involves assessing vendors' security practices, conducting due diligence, and ensuring that vendors adhere to security standards.

Regular data backups are critical for ensuring data availability in the event of data loss or ransomware attacks. Backups should be securely stored and regularly tested to ensure data integrity. Additionally, organizations should have a well-defined data recovery plan in case of data loss.

As organizations increasingly adopt cloud services, ensuring cloud security is paramount. Cloud security best practices include configuring cloud services securely, using strong authentication, encrypting data, and monitoring cloud environments for security threats.

When employees leave an organization, it's essential to have a process in place to revoke their access to systems and data promptly. Neglected access rights of former employees can pose a significant security risk.

Cybersecurity is not solely an IT concern; it requires the engagement of executives and leaders within an organization. Executives should be well-informed about cybersecurity risks and best practices to make informed decisions regarding cybersecurity investments and policies.

In a time when cyberthreats are always changing and becoming more sophisticated, cybersecurity best practices are the foundation of effective defense. Implementing a comprehensive set of practices, from employee training and secure access controls to encryption and incident response planning, is essential to protect against various threats. Cybersecurity requires constant attention to protect digital assets and keep up with new threats - it is not a one-time activity. By embracing these best practices, individuals and organizations alike can navigate the complex landscape of cybersecurity and fortify their defenses against the ever-present cyber threats that seek to exploit vulnerabilities in the digital realm.

Security policies and procedures

In an era of unprecedented reliance on digital technologies and the ever-expanding boundaries of cyberspace, the importance of robust security policies and procedures cannot be overstated. These policies and procedures are the backbone of an organization's cybersecurity posture, guiding its efforts to protect valuable assets, sensitive data, and critical systems. This section explores the multifaceted world of security policies and procedures, shedding light on their significance, components, development, implementation, and ongoing maintenance. From establishing a solid foundation through policy creation to the intricate details of procedures and their role in incident response, this discussion underscores the vital role that security policies and procedures play in safeguarding the digital frontier.

Security policies and procedures represent the guiding principles and tactical instructions that define how an organization approaches cybersecurity. They are not mere documents but living instruments that shape an organization's security culture. At their core, these documents serve several critical purposes. They help identify, assess, and mitigate risks to an organization's information assets, systems, and operations. They ensure adherence to regulatory requirements, industry standards, and legal obligations related to data protection and privacy. Policies and procedures consistently manage security across the organization, reducing the risk of ad-hoc or inconsistent practices. They provide a clear, standardized way to communicate security expectations, responsibilities, and practices to employees and stakeholders. Security procedures are pivotal in incident response, guiding the organization's actions during and after security incidents.

Effective security policies and procedures typically comprise several key components. Each policy begins with a clear and concise statement of its purpose and objectives. This sets the context for the policy and outlines its overarching goals. Policies define the scope of their applicability, specifying which assets, systems, or processes are covered. This ensures that policies are relevant and tailored to the organization's needs. Policies identify the roles and responsibilities of individuals or teams involved in implementing and adhering to the policy. This clarifies who is accountable for various aspects of security. Security policies establish specific requirements and standards that must be followed. These may include password complexity rules, encryption standards, and access control measures. Procedures provide step-by-step instructions for implementing the policy's requirements and standards. Guidelines are practical instructions that help employees perform security-related tasks correctly. Security procedures include incident response plans that detail how the organization should react to security incidents. This encompasses steps for detection, containment, investigation, and recovery.

Developing security policies and procedures is a meticulous process involving several key steps. Begin by conducting a extensive risk assessment to identify potential security threats and vulnerabilities. This forms the basis for determining the policies and procedures needed. Ensure that policies align with relevant laws and regulations, as non-compliance can result in legal consequences. Involve key stakeholders, including IT personnel, legal experts, compliance officers, and business leaders, to gather diverse perspectives and expertise in the policy development process. Develop policies and procedures clearly and concisely. Use language that is easily understandable by all employees, regardless of their technical background. Subject policies and procedures to rigorous review and seek input from relevant stakeholders. Before finalizing the documents, get approval from senior management or the board of directors. Once policies and procedures are established, conduct training sessions and awareness campaigns to educate employees and stakeholders about their contents and importance.

Effective implementation is essential for policies and procedures to have a meaningful impact. Clearly communicate the policies and procedures to all employees and stakeholders. Ensure that they understand the policies' importance and how they relate to their roles. Enforce compliance with policies and procedures through monitoring, audits, and regular assessments. Establish consequences for non-compliance, emphasizing the importance of security. Use technology solutions, such as access control systems and security software, to support the enforcement of policies and procedures. Once the threat is neutralized, procedures outline restoring affected systems and services to normal operations. This phase includes testing and validating system integrity. After the incident is resolved, a post-incident review is conducted. Procedures detail the steps for analyzing the incident's impact, identifying lessons learned, and updating security policies and procedures accordingly.

The world of cybersecurity is dynamic, with new threats and technologies continually emerging. Therefore, security policies and procedures must be subject to ongoing maintenance and review. Policies and procedures should be studied and updated on a regular manner to ensure they remain relevant and effective. New threats, technology updates, or changes in regulatory requirements may prompt changes. Implement continuous monitoring and assessment mechanisms to promptly detect and respond to security incidents. Ensure that incident response procedures remain effective. Provide continuous training and awareness programs to keep employees and stakeholders informed about changes in policies and procedures and emerging security threats. Conduct regular testing and drills to evaluate the organization's ability to execute security procedures effectively. This includes simulating various security incidents to test incident response capabilities.

In an interconnected digital landscape fraught with ever-evolving cyber threats, security policies and procedures are the cornerstone of effective cybersecurity. These documents provide the framework for identifying, assessing, and mitigating risks, ensuring regulatory compliance, and fostering a culture of security within organizations. From their development to implementation and ongoing maintenance, security policies and procedures are invaluable tools in safeguarding the digital frontier. Organizations that prioritize creating and enforcing robust security policies and procedures are better equipped to navigate the complex and ever-changing landscape of cybersecurity, fortifying their defenses against the myriad threats that seek to exploit vulnerabilities in the digital realm.

Security awareness training

In the ever-evolving landscape of cybersecurity threats, organizations face a formidable adversary: human error. Despite the most advanced security technologies and robust infrastructures, the actions and decisions of individuals within an organization can inadvertently expose it to cyber risks. This is where security awareness training plays a pivotal role. Security awareness training provides employees the knowledge and skills needed to determine, respond to, and mitigate cybersecurity threats. This section delves into the significance of security awareness training, explores its key components, examines strategies for effective implementation, and underscores its role in building a resilient human firewall.

Cybersecurity threats have become more sophisticated and pervasive than ever before. Phishing attacks, social engineering, malware, and other cyber threats often target the human element within an organization. Attackers exploit human vulnerabilities, such as ignorance or carelessness, to gain access to sensitive data, compromise systems, or perpetrate fraud. In this context, security awareness training emerges as a vital strategy to mitigate these risks.

One of the primary aims of security awareness training is to transform employees from potential security liabilities into vigilant and informed defenders of an organization's digital assets. By raising awareness about common cyber threats, teaching safe computing practices, and fostering a culture of cybersecurity, organizations can significantly reduce the human error factor and enhance their overall security posture.

Effective security awareness training encompasses several key components that ensure its relevance and impact:

Education and Awareness: Training programs should begin with foundational education and awareness-building. This includes introducing employees to the types of cyber threats they may encounter, the tactics employed by cybercriminals, and the potential consequences of security breaches. Creating a sense of urgency and importance is essential to capture employees' attention.

Phishing Awareness: Phishing attacks remain one of the most prevalent and effective cyber threats. Training should include specific modules on recognizing phishing emails, malicious attachments, and deceptive websites. Simulated phishing exercises can provide employees with real-world practice in identifying phishing attempts.

Secure Password Practices: Passwords are a critical aspect of cybersecurity. Training programs must instruct employees on how to create strong, unique passwords, the importance of not sharing passwords, and the benefits of using password management tools.

Social Engineering Awareness: Social engineering techniques like pretexting and baiting exploit human psychology. Security awareness training should educate employees about these tactics and guide how to verify the identity of individuals requesting sensitive information.

Device and Data Security: As employees increasingly use personal devices for work, training should cover device security, data encryption, and safe handling of sensitive information. Mobile device security is crucial, given the prevalence of smartphones and tablets in the workplace.

Reporting Procedures: Employees should be aware of how to report security incidents or suspicious activities. Clear reporting procedures ensure that potential threats are addressed promptly.

Regular Updates and Refreshers: Cyber threats evolve, so training content should be regularly updated to reflect new risks and vulnerabilities. Periodic refresher courses help reinforce knowledge and ensure that employees stay current with the latest security practices.

Compliance Awareness: Many industries have specific regulatory requirements related to data protection and privacy. Training programs should educate employees about these regulations and the organization's compliance obligations.

While the importance of security awareness training is evident, its effectiveness depends on the strategies employed during implementation. Tailored content that addresses employees' specific needs and roles is more likely to resonate with them. Interactive and engaging training, incorporating multimedia elements, quizzes, and real-world scenarios, captures and retains employees' attention. Continuous learning programs offer bite-sized, relevant content to employees throughout the year, reinforcing their knowledge and awareness.

Senior management support is vital for the success of security awareness training. Leaders should actively endorse and participate in training initiatives to set an example for employees. Conducting simulated phishing attacks and other security tests can assess employees' readiness and provide opportunities for teachable moments. Recognition and rewards for employees demonstrating exemplary security awareness practices can motivate others to remain vigilant. Gathering feedback from employees about the training program's effectiveness and areas for improvement helps refine the training content and delivery methods.

Measuring the impact of security awareness training is essential to gauge its effectiveness and make data-driven improvements. Key performance indicators (KPIs) that organizations can track include phishing resilience, incident reporting, security policy adherence, reduction in incidents, training completion rates, and employee feedback. These metrics provide insights into the program's effectiveness and allow organizations to tailor their training efforts accordingly.

Beyond training and awareness, cultivating a culture of cybersecurity is instrumental in fortifying the human firewall. A cybersecurity-aware culture is one where employees understand that security is everyone's responsibility and actively contribute to protecting the organization's digital assets. Leadership sets the tone for the organization's culture. When leaders prioritize and exemplify cybersecurity practices, employees are more likely to follow suit. Effective communication ensures that security expectations are clear, and employees understand their role in maintaining security. Continuous reinforcement, through ongoing training, reminders, and recognition, keeps cybersecurity at the forefront of employees' minds.

Security awareness training is a critical defense mechanism in a digital landscape fraught with ever-evolving cyber threats. By educating employees, raising awareness about cyber risks, and fostering a culture of cybersecurity, organizations can significantly reduce the human error factor in cybersecurity incidents. Security awareness training is not a one-time effort but an ongoing commitment to keep employees informed and vigilant in the face of evolving threats. As the digital realm expands, the importance of security awareness training in fortifying the human firewall becomes increasingly evident, ensuring that employees are not the weakest link but an essential part of the defense against cyberattacks.

CHAPTER VIII

Case Studies in Ethical Hacking

Real-world case studies of ethical hacking successes

Ethical hacking, or penetration testing or white-hat hacking, is a practice where cybersecurity professionals use their skills to determine vulnerabilities and weaknesses in computer systems, networks, and applications. These experts are critical in helping organizations strengthen their cybersecurity defenses by finding and addressing security flaws before malicious hackers can exploit them. In this section, we explore real- world case studies of ethical hacking successes, showcasing instances where ethical hackers have significantly impacted safeguarding digital assets, protecting sensitive data, and thwarting cyber threats.

The United States Department of Defense (DoD) safeguards an extensive network of sensitive military and government systems. To test the security of its infrastructure, the DoD initiated the "Hack the Pentagon" program. Under this program, ethical hackers were invited to uncover vulnerabilities in DoD websites and systems. The first challenge, known as DEFCON, attracted over 1,400 ethical hackers.

The program's success was immediate and profound. Ethical hackers discovered 138 vulnerabilities, all promptly patched by the DoD's cybersecurity team. The program's effectiveness and the collaboration between ethical hackers and the government demonstrated the power of harnessing external expertise to bolster security. This initiative protected critical government systems and showcased the importance of ethical hacking in strengthening national security.

In 2013, one of the most significant data breaches in retail history occurred when cybercriminals stole millions of Target customers' credit card information and personal data. This breach led to severe financial losses and damage to Target's reputation. Target took an unconventional approach to regain trust and prevent future attacks by hiring renowned cybersecurity expert Brian Krebs.

Brian Krebs, a respected investigative journalist with expertise in cybersecurity, was effectively acting as an ethical hacker. He meticulously investigated the breach, traced the attack's origins, and shared his findings with Target. His efforts helped Target identify the vulnerabilities exploited by the attackers and contributed to the arrest and prosecution of those responsible.

This case demonstrates that ethical hacking doesn't always occur within the confines of traditional cybersecurity roles. By leveraging external expertise and unconventional methods, organizations can identify and rectify vulnerabilities, mitigating the damage caused by cyberattacks.

Several major technology companies have embraced the concept of bug bounty programs, inviting ethical hackers to find and report vulnerabilities in their software and platforms. One notable example is Google's Vulnerability Reward Program (VRP), which rewards ethical hackers for identifying and reporting security flaws in Google products.

In one instance, a British ethical hacker, Tomasz Bojarski, discovered a critical vulnerability in Google's Cloud Platform. This vulnerability could have allowed attackers to take control of customer applications and data. Bojarski reported the flaw to Google, which promptly addressed the issue and awarded him a substantial bug bounty. This case highlights the symbiotic relationship between ethical hackers and organizations, where hackers' skills are put to constructive use, and organizations benefit from enhanced security.

In 2015, ethical hackers Charlie Miller and Chris Valasek made headlines when they demonstrated a remote hack of a Jeep Cherokee's control systems. Their research revealed alarming vulnerabilities that could potentially compromise the safety of vehicles and passengers. Rather than exploiting these flaws for malicious purposes, they responsibly disclosed their findings to Fiat Chrysler Automobiles (FCA).

FCA took the issue seriously and issued a recall to fix the vulnerabilities, ensuring the safety of millions of vehicles on the road. This case exemplifies the critical role ethical hackers play in protecting digital assets and physical safety. It serves as a reminder that ethical hacking extends beyond the digital realm, with implications for the security of the physical world.

One of the most well-known credit reporting companies in the world, Equifax, experienced a significant data breach in 2017 that resulted in the exposure of 147 million people's private information. After the breach was discovered, Equifax took extensive measures to investigate and remediate the situation.

As part of their response, Equifax engaged the services of ethical hacking experts to conduct a thorough post-incident analysis. These experts scrutinized the breach, identified the exploited vulnerabilities, and recommended improving security. Their involvement helped Equifax understand the root causes of the breach and implement comprehensive security enhancements to prevent future incidents.

This case underscores the importance of ethical hacking in proactively identifying vulnerabilities and learning from security incidents to prevent recurrence.

In the realm of space exploration, where the stakes are incredibly high, cybersecurity is of paramount importance. In collaboration with NASA, SpaceX recognized the need to secure its systems against potential cyber threats. To ensure the safety and success of space missions, they engaged ethical hackers to test their systems rigorously.

The ethical hackers conducted thorough assessments, identified vulnerabilities, and worked closely with SpaceX and NASA to remediate the issues. This collaborative effort between private companies, government agencies, and ethical hackers highlights the critical role ethical hacking plays in protecting digital assets and human lives in high-stakes environments.

In a unique and proactive approach to cybersecurity, the Indian government initiated the "Hack the Airwaves" program. This program invited ethical hackers to assess the security of the country's satellite communications systems. The goal was to identify vulnerabilities that hostile actors could potentially exploit.

The program was a resounding success, with ethical hackers uncovering and responsibly disclosing vulnerabilities in India's satellite communication infrastructure. The government promptly addressed these issues, enhancing the security of critical communication systems. This innovative initiative demonstrates how governments can harness the expertise of ethical hackers to safeguard national security assets.

Real-world case studies of ethical hacking successes underscore ethical hackers' pivotal role in securing digital assets, protecting sensitive data, and mitigating cyber threats. From government agencies and major corporations to automotive companies and space exploration endeavors, organizations of all types and sizes recognize the value of ethical hacking in bolstering their cybersecurity defenses.

These cases highlight the versatility of ethical hacking, showcasing how it can be employed proactively to identify vulnerabilities, reactively to investigate breaches, and collaboratively to strengthen security postures. Ethical hackers are not adversaries but allies in the ongoing battle against cyber threats, working tirelessly to safeguard digital landscapes, critical infrastructure, and even human lives.

As the cyber threat landscape evolves, the successes of ethical hacking serve as a testament to the power of ethical hackers in fortifying our digital world. Their efforts exemplify the principle that knowledge and skill, when wielded responsibly, can be formidable weapons against cyber adversaries, ultimately ensuring a safer and more secure digital future.

Lessons learned from each case

Real-world ethical hacking successes provide valuable insights into the evolving landscape of cybersecurity and offer essential lessons that organizations and individuals can learn from. In this section, we delve into the lessons gleaned from each of the previously discussed case studies, highlighting the key takeaways that can help bolster cybersecurity practices and inform decision-making in the face of ever-evolving cyber threats.

The DEFCON Challenge undertaken by the United States Department of Defense (DoD) illustrates several crucial lessons. Firstly, it emphasizes the significance of proactive security testing and collaboration with external experts. By inviting ethical hackers to assess their systems, the DoD embraced a transparent and collaborative approach to cybersecurity. Organizations should recognize that security is a collective effort, and external perspectives can uncover vulnerabilities that internal teams may overlook.

Secondly, the DoD's swift response to identified vulnerabilities demonstrates the importance of prompt remediation. Cyber threats evolve rapidly, and vulnerabilities must be addressed without delay. Regular security assessments and quick action are key to staying ahead of potential attackers.

Lastly, the DEFCON Challenge showcases the role of ethical hacking in national security. Government agencies should harness the expertise of ethical hackers to safeguard critical infrastructure and sensitive data, recognizing that the digital realm is an integral component of modern national defense.

The Target data breach case underscores the importance of post-breach ethical hacking and unconventional approaches to cybersecurity. Organizations should not limit their response to traditional methods but be open to seeking external expertise, as exemplified by Target's collaboration with investigative journalist Brian Krebs.

This case also highlights the severe consequences of failing to secure customer data adequately. The financial and reputational damage incurred by Target serves as a stark warning to organizations worldwide. Prioritizing data protection, encryption, and incident response preparedness is essential.

Lastly, Brian Krebs' role in the Target case demonstrates that ethical hacking can take various forms. Cybersecurity professionals may operate in unconventional roles and should be encouraged to use their skills for the greater good. Ethical hacking can be a potent tool for discovering vulnerabilities and responding to security incidents.

Bug bounty programs, such as Google's Vulnerability Reward Program (VRP), highlight the benefits of collaboration between organizations and ethical hackers. These programs demonstrate that ethical hackers can be valuable allies rather than adversaries.

One key lesson from bug bounty programs is that organizations can incentivize ethical hackers to report vulnerabilities responsibly. Rewarding hackers for their efforts encourages them to identify and disclose flaws rather than exploiting them for malicious purposes. Organizations should consider implementing such programs to harness external expertise and enhance security.

Furthermore, bug bounty programs emphasize the importance of continuous monitoring and improvement. Cyber threats evolve, and organizations must adapt to stay ahead. Regularly updating and expanding bug bounty programs ensures that security is an ongoing process, not a one-time effort.

The Jeep Cherokee hack case offers critical insights into the intersection of cybersecurity and physical safety. It underscores the need for rigorous security testing in industries where lives are at stake, such as automotive and healthcare.

One lesson is that security vulnerabilities can have far-reaching consequences. Organizations must prioritize data security and the physical safety of their products and users. This involves conducting thorough security assessments and promptly addressing identified flaws.

Additionally, Charlie Miller and Chris Valasek's responsible disclosure of their findings highlights the ethical aspect of hacking. Ethical hackers prioritize public safety and accountable reporting, distinguishing themselves from malicious hackers who exploit vulnerabilities for personal gain. This case emphasizes the importance of ethical considerations in the cybersecurity field.

The Equifax breach case underscores the significance of post-incident ethical hacking and lessons learned. Organizations that experience security breaches should conduct thorough investigations and leverage ethical hacking expertise to understand the root causes.

One lesson is that transparency and accountability are crucial during and after a security breach. Equifax's response included engaging ethical hackers to help identify vulnerabilities and prevent future incidents. Open communication with affected parties and stakeholders is essential to rebuilding trust.

Furthermore, organizations should view security incidents as opportunities for improvement. Equifax's post-breach ethical hacking efforts allowed them to strengthen their security posture and prevent similar breaches in the future. Learning from mistakes and actively addressing vulnerabilities are vital components of a resilient cybersecurity strategy.

The collaboration between SpaceX, NASA, and ethical hackers emphasizes securing critical infrastructure, even in high-stakes environments like space exploration. Lessons from this case include recognizing that no organization is immune to cyber threats, regardless of its mission or industry.

One lesson is that proactive security testing is essential for safeguarding complex systems. Space missions involve intricate technology, and vulnerabilities can have catastrophic consequences. Ethical hackers can help identify and address these vulnerabilities before malicious actors can exploit them.

Additionally, the collaboration highlights the value of partnerships between public and private sectors.

Government agencies, private companies, and ethical hackers can work together to enhance security and protect critical infrastructure. Public-private collaboration is increasingly vital in the face of advanced cyber threats.

The "Hack the Airwaves" program initiated by the Indian government offers a unique perspective on cybersecurity. It emphasizes the importance of securing communication infrastructure, particularly in national security.

One key lesson is that governments can benefit from external expertise in securing critical infrastructure. Ethical hackers can identify vulnerabilities that may otherwise go unnoticed. Governments should actively engage with ethical hackers to enhance their cybersecurity defenses.

This initiative also highlights the value of unconventional approaches to cybersecurity. Governments should be open to innovative ideas and initiatives that can bolster national security. Cybersecurity is dynamic, and creative solutions are essential in protecting critical assets. Real-

world ethical hacking successes provide a wealth of lessons organizations and individuals can apply to enhance cybersecurity practices. These lessons encompass the importance of proactive security testing, collaboration with ethical hackers, swift remediation of vulnerabilities, transparency in the face of security incidents, and prioritizing data and physical safety.

Moreover, these cases demonstrate the ethical aspect of hacking, showcasing that ethical hackers prioritize public safety and responsible reporting. Their expertise can be harnessed to strengthen security, prevent breaches, and protect critical infrastructure.

As cyber threats continue to evolve, the lessons from real-world ethical hacking successes guide organizations and governments alike. The knowledge gained from these cases can inform strategies, policies, and decision- making, ultimately contributing to a more secure digital landscape. Ethical hacking is not only a valuable tool for identifying vulnerabilities but also a force for positive change in the realm of cybersecurity, promoting responsible and effective security practices.

Ethical considerations in these cases

The realm of ethical hacking is characterized not only by technical prowess but also by a strong ethical framework that guides the actions of cybersecurity professionals. As we examine real-world ethical hacking successes, it becomes apparent that ethical considerations are at the heart of these endeavors. In this section, we explore the ethical dimensions of each case study, highlighting the principles and values that underpin the actions of ethical hackers and organizations in their pursuit of cybersecurity excellence.

In the DEFCON Challenge initiated by the United States Department of Defense (DoD), ethical considerations are central to the program's success. The collaboration between the DoD and ethical hackers is founded on the principles of transparency, responsibility, and shared commitment to national security.

Ethical hackers who participate in the DEFCON Challenge comply to a stringent code of ethics that prioritizes the responsible disclosure of vulnerabilities. Their aim is not to exploit weaknesses but to strengthen the security of critical government systems. This commitment to responsible hacking aligns with the principle of beneficence, where ethical hackers use their skills for the greater good, protecting the nation's digital infrastructure.

From an organizational perspective, the DoD's decision to engage ethical hackers reflects its commitment to transparency and the recognition that external expertise is a valuable asset in maintaining national security. The ethical consideration here is one of accountability, with the DoD taking responsibility for protecting its systems and actively seeking to identify and address vulnerabilities.

Investigative journalist Brian Krebs' activities following the Target data leak were heavily influenced by ethical considerations. Krebs's decision to investigate the breach and share his findings with Target exemplifies the ethical principle of accountability.

Brian Krebs acted as a responsible and conscientious whistleblower, highlighting the breach's severity and its implications for the public. His commitment to transparency and truth-telling aligns with ethical journalism practices and underscores the importance of holding organizations accountable for security lapses.

From Target's perspective, the ethical considerations revolved around taking responsibility for the breach, promptly addressing vulnerabilities, and ensuring the security of customer data. Target's response demonstrated its commitment to rectify the situation and prevent future incidents, aligning with ethical principles of duty and responsibility.

Bug bounty programs, like Google's Vulnerability Reward Program (VRP), are built upon collaboration and mutual benefit principles. Ethical hackers who participate in these programs are motivated by financial rewards and the ethical consideration of responsible disclosure.

The ethical dimension of bug bounty programs lies in the responsible reporting of vulnerabilities. Ethical hackers must promptly disclose their findings to the organization and work collaboratively to address the issues. This principle of responsible hacking promotes transparency, accountability, and the shared goal of improving security.

Organizations that implement bug bounty programs recognize the value of external expertise in strengthening security. Their ethical considerations involve fostering a collaborative environment where ethical hackers are treated as partners rather than adversaries. This approach aligns with principles of fairness and respect for the ethical hacker's role.

The Jeep Cherokee hack case raises profound ethical questions about the intersection of cybersecurity and public safety. Ethical hackers Charlie Miller and Chris Valasek conducted their research with the utmost responsibility and accountability.

Their decision to responsibly disclose the vulnerabilities they uncovered reflects a commitment to the ethical principle of non-maleficence, ensuring that their actions did not harm the public. By sharing their findings with Fiat Chrysler Automobiles (FCA) and the public, they contributed to public safety.

From FCA's perspective, the ethical consideration revolved around promptly addressing the vulnerabilities to protect the safety of vehicle occupants. FCA recognized its duty to ensure the security of its products, and its response aligned with ethical principles of responsibility and accountability.

In the wake of the Equifax breach, ethical considerations were critical in the post-incident response. Responsible and in-depth investigations were carried out by ethical hackers hired by Equifax to identify the primary causes of the breach.

Ethical principles of accountability and transparency guided their actions. Equifax recognized its responsibility to affected individuals and stakeholders and took steps to rebuild trust through open communication and remediation efforts.

The ethical dimension of this case extends to the broader cybersecurity community. The lessons learned from the Equifax breach underscore the importance of sharing knowledge and collaborating to prevent future incidents. Organizations and ethical hackers alike have an obligation to improve the overall security of the digital environment.

The collaboration between SpaceX, NASA, and ethical hackers highlights the ethical consideration of safeguarding human lives in high-stakes environments. SpaceX and NASA recognized their ethical duty to protect space missions from cyber threats.

Ethical hackers engaged in this collaboration adhere to principles of responsibility and beneficence, using their expertise to ensure the safety of astronauts and mission success. Their actions are driven by a commitment to the ethical principles of non-maleficence and justice, ensuring that space exploration remains safe and secure.

This case underscores the ethical responsibility of organizations involved in critical endeavors to prioritize cybersecurity and collaborate with ethical hackers to identify vulnerabilities. It also emphasizes the broader ethical consideration of protecting human lives in the digital age.

The "Hack the Airwaves" program initiated by the Indian government presents a unique ethical perspective in the context of national security. Ethical hackers who participated in this program recognized their ethical duty to safeguard critical communication infrastructure.

Their actions align with the principles of beneficence and responsibility, contributing to protecting national security assets. The Indian government's ethical consideration was to proactively identify and address vulnerabilities to prevent potential threats.

This initiative demonstrates that governments can embrace ethical hacking to enhance national security while adhering to ethical principles of transparency, accountability, and the greater good.

Ethical considerations are the foundation upon which real-world ethical hacking successes are built. From responsible disclosure to transparency, accountability, and a commitment to the greater good, ethical principles guide the actions of ethical hackers and organizations alike.

The ethical necessity of cybersecurity is shown by the lessons that may be drawn from these cases. In an increasingly interconnected and digitized world, ethical hacking is a powerful force for positive change, promoting responsible and ethical practices that enhance security, protect data, and safeguard public safety. As the cybersecurity landscape evolves, ethical considerations will remain central to the ethical hacker's mission of securing the digital realm.

CHAPTER IX

Career Opportunities in Ethical Hacking

Exploring the job market for ethical hackers

In today's hyperconnected world, the digital landscape is rife with vulnerabilities that cybercriminals exploit to compromise systems, steal data, and wreak havoc. As a result, organizations across industries recognize the critical need to fortify their cybersecurity defenses. Ethical hackers, also known as white-hat hackers or penetration testers, play a pivotal role in this endeavor. They are cybersecurity professionals who leverage their expertise to determine vulnerabilities in networks, systems, and applications before malicious hackers can exploit them. This section delves into the dynamic job market for ethical hackers, exploring the growing demand for their skills, the diverse career paths available, the requisite qualifications, and the factors driving this field's evolution.

The need for ethical hackers has increased dramatically in recent years, and this trend doesn't appear to be slowing down. Several factors contribute to the growing need for these cybersecurity experts. Escalating cyber threats, regulatory compliance requirements, and high-profile breaches have all heightened the demand for skilled ethical hackers. Cyber threats, including phishing attacks, ransomware, and data breaches, have become increasingly sophisticated. Organizations require experts who can proactively identify vulnerabilities and shore up defenses. Data protection regulations, like GDPR and

HIPAA, have placed stringent demands on organizations. Compliance with these regulations necessitates robust cybersecurity measures, driving the demand for ethical hackers. High-profile data breaches, like those affecting Equifax and Target, have underscored the devastating consequences of security lapses. These incidents have prompted organizations to invest in cybersecurity, fueling the demand for ethical hackers.

Ethical hacking offers diverse career paths, each catering to different interests and skill sets. These paths include penetration testers, security consultants, security analysts, Certified Ethical Hackers (CEH), and bug bounty hunters. Penetration testers simulate cyberattacks to identify vulnerabilities, while security consultants guide enhancing cybersecurity. Security analysts monitor networks for security incidents, and CEHs possess specialized training and certification. Bug bounty hunters participate in programs that reward the discovery of vulnerabilities. These varied roles ensure that ethical hackers can find a niche that meets their skills and interests.

Entering the field of ethical hacking typically requires a combination of education, certifications, and hands-on experience. Many ethical hackers hold computer science, information technology, or cybersecurity degrees. However, formal education is not always a strict requirement, and individuals with strong technical aptitude may enter the field through alternative pathways. Certifications like Certified Ethical Hacker (CEH), Certified Information Systems Security Professional (CISSP), Certified Information Security Manager (CISM), and Offensive Security Certified Professional (OSCP) serve as benchmarks of expertise. Proficiency in programming languages like Python, knowledge of network protocols, and experience with penetration testing tools are highly valuable. Strong analytical skills for assessing complex systems and effective communication skills for reporting findings to non-technical stakeholders are also essential.

The job market for ethical hackers continues to evolve in response to emerging technologies and cybersecurity challenges. Factors driving this evolution include the proliferation of Internet of Things (IoT) devices and cloud computing, AI-driven cyberattacks, changes in data protection regulations, heightened cybersecurity awareness, and the challenges introduced by remote work. Ethical hackers are increasingly tasked with assessing the security of IoT ecosystems, cloud-based infrastructure, and combatting AI-powered threats. They also help organizations comply with evolving data protection and privacy regulations, avoid fines for data breaches, and secure remote work environments in response to the COVID-19 pandemic.

In conclusion, the job market for ethical hackers is vibrant and shows no signs of slowing down. As cyber threats evolve and organizations prioritize cybersecurity, the demand for skilled ethical hackers will only increase. The diverse career paths, requisite qualifications, and dynamic nature of the field make ethical hacking an appealing and rewarding career choice for those passionate about securing the digital realm. Ethical hackers serve as the vanguard of cybersecurity, helping organizations stay ahead of cybercriminals and safeguarding the digital landscape for generations to come.

Required skills and certifications

Ethical hackers serve as the frontline defenders of digital systems and networks in the ever-evolving cybersecurity landscape. They aim to proactively identify vulnerabilities, assess security measures, and fortify defenses against cyber threats. Ethical hackers must possess a formidable combination of skills, knowledge, and certifications to excel in this role. In this section, we explore the essential skills that ethical hackers must acquire and the certifications that validate their expertise. These foundational elements equip them with the capabilities needed to navigate the complex world of ethical hacking.

At the core of an ethical hacker's skill set is technical proficiency. They must deeply understand various technical domains, including networking, operating systems, programming, cybersecurity tools, and web technologies. This knowledge enables them to analyze network traffic, identify network infrastructure vulnerabilities, and assess communication channel security. Proficiency in programming languages like Python is essential for scripting, automation, and custom tool development. Ethical hackers also rely on various cybersecurity tools for tasks such as network scanning, vulnerability assessment, and intrusion detection.

In addition to technical proficiency, ethical hackers must understand networking principles and technologies in-depth. This knowledge enables them to assess network security effectively, identify vulnerabilities, and develop strategies to mitigate risks. Ethical hackers should comprehend concepts like subnetting, routing, firewall configurations, and VPN protocols. Furthermore, they need to be skilled in analyzing network traffic patterns, which can reveal potential security issues or suspicious activities.

A solid foundation in cybersecurity fundamentals is indispensable for ethical hackers. They should be well-versed in key concepts such as threat modeling, risk assessment, encryption, access control, and security policies. Understanding the cybersecurity landscape, including different attack vectors and common vulnerabilities, is essential for anticipating and countering potential threats. Ethical hackers must also be knowledgeable about industry-standard security frameworks and best practices.

Ethical hackers are essentially digital detectives. They must have a strong analytical and problem-solving skills to dissect complex systems, identify vulnerabilities, and devise effective solutions. Analytical thinking allows them to assess security risks methodically and prioritize remediation efforts. Ethical hackers often encounter novel challenges, requiring creative problem-solving to develop unique solutions to emerging threats.

Effective communication is a non-negotiable skill for ethical hackers. They must be capable of conveying complex technical findings and recommendations to technical as well as non-technical stakeholders. Reporting vulnerabilities, explaining potential risks, and justifying security improvements demand clear and concise communication. Ethical hackers also play a critical role in educating organizations about cybersecurity best practices, making effective communication a vital skill.

Certifications serve as industry-recognized benchmarks of expertise for ethical hackers. They validate the individual's knowledge and skills, making them highly sought after in the job market. Some of the most prominent certifications for ethical hackers include the Certified Ethical Hacker (CEH), Certified Information Systems Security Professional (CISSP), Offensive Security Certified Professional (OSCP), Certified Information Security Manager (CISM), CompTIA Security+, and Certified Security Analyst (ECSA). These certifications demonstrate an individual's competence in assessing and securing systems, enhancing their credibility and employability in cybersecurity.

In conclusion, ethical hackers are pivotal in defending digital systems and networks from cyber threats. To excel in this profession, they must cultivate diverse skills encompassing technical proficiency, networking knowledge, cybersecurity fundamentals, analytical and problem-solving abilities, and effective communication. Additionally, certifications validate their expertise and enhance their credibility in the cybersecurity field. As the cybersecurity landscape evolves, ethical hackers must remain dedicated to lifelong learning and skill development to stay ahead of emerging challenges and threats.

Building a career in ethical hacking

The world of ethical hacking, often referred to as "white-hat hacking," represents a dynamic and rapidly evolving field within the realm of cybersecurity. Ethical hackers are the digital defenders of the modern age, tasked with identifying vulnerabilities in computer systems, networks, and applications to protect organizations from malicious cyber threats. As the frequency and advancement of cyberattacks continue to rise, the demand for skilled ethical hackers has reached unprecedented levels. In this section, we explore the journey of building a career in ethical hacking, including the essential steps, educational pathways, requisite skills, and the evolving landscape of this exciting profession.

To embark on a career in ethical hacking, one must first understand the role and responsibilities of an ethical hacker. Unlike malicious hackers, ethical hackers operate explicitly to enhance security. Their primary mission is to identify vulnerabilities and weaknesses in digital systems before malicious actors can exploit them. Ethical hackers employ various techniques, tools, and methodologies to assess the security posture of organizations and help them shore up their defenses. This role is crucial in safeguarding sensitive data, protecting against cyber threats, and ensuring the resilience of digital infrastructure.

A career in ethical hacking typically begins with a strong educational foundation. While formal education is not always a strict requirement, it provides an essential framework for understanding computer science, information technology, and cybersecurity principles. Common educational pathways include bachelor's and master's degrees in fields like cybersecurity, information technology, computer science, or related disciplines. These programs provide a structured curriculum covering essential computer systems, networking, programming, and cybersecurity topics. Additionally, online courses and bootcamps offer flexible and focused training in ethical hacking, providing valuable alternatives to traditional academic programs. Certifications also play a pivotal role in the education of ethical hackers. Industry-recognized certifications like Certified Ethical Hacker (CEH), Certified Information Systems Security Professional (CISSP), Offensive Security Certified Professional (OSCP), and Certified Information Security Manager (CISM) validate a candidate's knowledge and skills in ethical hacking and cybersecurity.

Education alone does not suffice in the field of ethical hacking. Ethical hackers must cultivate diverse skills to excel in their roles. These skills include technical proficiency, networking knowledge, cybersecurity fundamentals, analytical and problem-solving abilities, and effective communication. Technical proficiency encompasses a deep understanding of operating systems, networking protocols, programming languages, and cybersecurity tools. Proficiency in scripting languages like Python is particularly valuable for automation and custom tool development. Networking knowledge involves concepts like routing, switching, firewalls, and network security protocols, which are essential for assessing network security effectively. Understanding cybersecurity fundamentals is crucial for threat modeling, risk assessment, encryption, access control, and security policies. Ethical hackers also require strong analytical and problem-solving skills to dissect complex systems, assess security risks, and prioritize remediation efforts. Effective communication is vital for reporting vulnerabilities, presenting findings to stakeholders, and educating organizations about cybersecurity best practices.

Practical experience is invaluable in the world of ethical hacking. It provides hands-on exposure to real-world scenarios, challenges, and vulnerabilities. Aspiring ethical hackers can gain practical experience through various means, including Capture The Flag (CTF) challenges, virtual labs, internships, entry-level positions, and bug bounty programs. CTF challenges are cybersecurity competitions that involve solving puzzles, cracking codes, and exploiting vulnerabilities in controlled environments. Virtual labs allow individuals to practice ethical hacking techniques in a safe and controlled environment, offering hands-on experience with various tools and scenarios. Internships, junior security analyst roles, and helpdesk positions provide on-the-job experience in cybersecurity and IT departments. Bug bounty programs reward ethical hackers for discovering and responsibly disclosing security vulnerabilities in organizations' systems, offering a real-world avenue for applying their skills.

Ethical hacking certifications are highly regarded in the industry and can significantly enhance an individual's career prospects. These certifications validate a candidate's knowledge and practical skills in ethical hacking. Some of the notable certifications include Certified Ethical Hacker (or CEH), Offensive Security Certified Professional (or OSCP), Certified Information Systems Security Professional (or CISSP), and Certified Information Security Manager (or CISM). These certifications demonstrate an individual's competence in assessing and securing systems, enhancing their credibility and employability in cybersecurity.

The career pathways in ethical hacking are diverse and offer numerous opportunities for specialization. Common career paths include penetration testers (pen testers), security consultants, security analysts, Certified Ethical Hackers (CEHs), and bug bounty hunters. Penetration testers simulate cyberattacks on an organization's systems to identify vulnerabilities, employing techniques like network scanning, vulnerability assessments, and social engineering tests. Security consultants guide organizations on enhancing their overall cybersecurity posture, conducting risk assessments, developing security strategies, and recommending security solutions. Security analysts monitor an organization's network and systems for security incidents, investigating breaches, analyzing security data, and developing strategies to mitigate threats. CEHs have completed specialized training and passed the CEH exam, possessing a broad range of skills and knowledge valuable to organizations seeking to secure their digital assets. Bug bounty hunters participate in bug bounty programs organizations offer, earning rewards for discovering and responsibly disclosing security vulnerabilities.

The field of ethical hacking is in a constant state of flux, with new threats, technologies, and attack vectors emerging regularly. As such, ethical hackers must commit to continuous learning and professional development. Staying current with industry trends, attending cybersecurity conferences, and participating in relevant training programs are essential for maintaining proficiency. Ethical hackers also operate within a framework of strict ethical guidelines. They must adhere to a code of ethics emphasizing responsible and legal hacking practices, obtain proper authorization before conducting penetration tests, report vulnerabilities to the affected parties, and protect the privacy and confidentiality of sensitive data.

Building a career in ethical hacking is a rewarding and intellectually stimulating journey. As organizations increasingly recognize the importance of robust cybersecurity measures, the demand for ethical hackers grows. To succeed in this field, individuals must acquire a solid educational foundation, cultivate essential skills, gain practical experience, earn relevant certifications, and stay adaptable in the face of evolving threats. Ethical hackers play a crucial role in safeguarding digital ecosystems, making their contributions indispensable in our increasingly interconnected world.

CHAPTER X

The Future of Cybersecurity

Emerging technologies and threats

The cybersecurity landscape is in perpetual motion, responding to the evolving technologies that drive our digital age. As society becomes more reliant on technology, the potential risks and threats to our digital assets and privacy continue to expand. To effectively defend against these threats, cybersecurity professionals must stay ahead of the curve, anticipating new challenges and adapting to emerging technologies. In this section, we explore some of the key emerging technologies and threats in the field of cybersecurity, shedding light on the ongoing battle to secure our digital world.

Machine Learning (or ML) and Artificial Intelligence (or AI) have rapidly emerged as dual-edged swords in the realm of cybersecurity. On one hand, AI and ML technologies are being harnessed to bolster security measures, helping to identify and respond to threats with unprecedented speed and accuracy. AI-powered systems can analyze vast datasets to detect anomalies, predict potential breaches, and automate attack responses. However, on the other hand, cybercriminals are also leveraging AI and ML to develop sophisticated attacks that can adapt and evolve in real-time. For instance, AI-driven malware can mutate to avoid detection, making it more challenging for traditional security solutions to keep up.

The Internet of Things (IoT) devices proliferation has introduced a new frontier of vulnerabilities. IoT devices, ranging from smart thermostats and cameras to industrial control systems, often lack robust security measures. These devices are frequently interconnected and communicate with other devices and networks, creating potential entry points for cyberattacks. As the number of IoT devices grows, so does the attack surface for cybercriminals. Protecting these devices and the data they handle presents a significant challenge in modern cybersecurity.

While quantum computing holds immense promise for solving complex problems, it also substantially threatens existing encryption methods. Quantum computers have the potential to break widely used encryption algorithms, such as RSA and ECC, by quickly factoring large numbers. As quantum computing matures, the encryption mechanisms that underpin secure communications and data protection will need to evolve to resist these new threats. Post-quantum cryptography is an emerging field that aims to develop encryption algorithms resilient to quantum attacks.

Ransomware attacks have evolved from mere data encryption to data theft and extortion. In addition to encrypting files and requiring a ransom for decryption, cybercriminals now often exfiltrate sensitive data before locking it down. They then threaten to release or sell this data if the ransom is not paid, adding a new layer of urgency and complexity to these attacks. Ransomware-as-a-Service (RaaS) has also become a thriving underground business model, allowing even non-technical criminals to execute ransomware attacks.

Supply chain attacks involve targeting third-party vendors, service providers, or software developers to compromise their customers' or partners' systems and networks. Attackers infiltrate the supply chain to deliver malicious code or tampered software updates, which can then be unknowingly distributed to various organizations. Notable supply chain attacks, like the SolarWinds breach, have demonstrated the scale and sophistication of this threat.

Attackers exploit zero-day vulnerabilities before the software vendor becomes knowledgeable of them and releases a patch. These vulnerabilities can be highly valuable to cybercriminals because no known defenses or fixes exist. Identifying and mitigating zero-day vulnerabilities is a constant challenge for cybersecurity professionals, as attackers constantly seek new weaknesses to exploit.

Deepfake technology, which uses AI to create realistic-looking but entirely fabricated videos or audio recordings, presents a significant threat in the realm of social engineering. Attackers can use deepfakes to impersonate trusted individuals or manipulate media content to deceive targets. Deepfake-based phishing attacks can be compelling, making it challenging for individuals and organizations to distinguish between genuine and fake communications.

The widespread adoption of cloud computing has redefined the cybersecurity landscape. While cloud providers offer robust security measures, the shared responsibility model means that customers are in charge of securing their data and applications in the cloud. Common cloud-related security issues are misconfigurations, weak access controls, and insecure APIs. Ensuring the security of cloud environments needs a holistic approach that combines proper configurations, monitoring, and user training.

The rollout of 5G networks brings both benefits and challenges to cybersecurity. While 5G offers faster and more reliable connectivity, it also expands the attack surface due to the increased number of connected devices and the potential for more extensive use of IoT. 5G networks' increased bandwidth and decreased latency could potentially make distributed denial-of-service (DDoS) assaults more effective and swift.

Organizations worldwide have compliance issues due to the constantly changing data privacy requirements, such as the California Consumer Privacy Act (CCPA) and the General Data Protection Regulation of the European Union. Strict data management and strong security measures are necessary to maintain compliance with these standards. Failing to do so may result in hefty fines and harm to one's reputation.

In conclusion, the field of cybersecurity is in a constant state of flux, shaped by emerging technologies and evolving threats. As AI and ML enhance both security and cyberattack capabilities, cybersecurity professionals must harness these tools to stay ahead of cybercriminals. The vulnerabilities introduced by IoT, quantum computing, and supply chain attacks demand proactive mitigation strategies. The evolution of ransomware, zero-day vulnerabilities, and social engineering tactics underscores the need for continuous vigilance and user education. Cloud security, 5G networks, and changing regulatory landscapes add further complexity to cybersecurity. To navigate these challenges successfully, cybersecurity professionals must remain adaptable, innovative, and committed to protecting the digital world from emerging threats.

Predictions for the future of cybersecurity

The world of cybersecurity is in a perpetual state of evolution, driven by quick advancements in technology and an ever-expanding digital landscape. As we look to the future, it becomes increasingly clear that the field of cybersecurity will face new challenges and opportunities. In this section, we explore several key predictions for the future of cybersecurity, offering insights into how the industry will adapt to emerging threats and technologies.

Artificial Intelligence (or AI) will continue to be pivotal in the future of cybersecurity. On one hand, AI-powered cybersecurity systems will become more sophisticated and capable of identifying and mitigating threats in real-time. Machine learning algorithms will be instrumental in analyzing vast datasets to detect anomalies and predict potential breaches. AI-driven threat intelligence will empower organizations to defend against cyberattacks proactively.

However, the same AI technologies will also be harnessed by cybercriminals to develop more advanced and evasive attack methods. AI-powered malware and automated hacking tools will significantly challenge traditional cybersecurity defenses. This AI arms race will require cybersecurity professionals to continuously refine their skills and adopt innovative approaches to stay ahead of malicious actors.

The advent of quantum computing will present a fundamental shift in the field of cryptography. Quantum computers have the potential to break widely used encryption algorithms, rendering existing cryptographic methods obsolete. As a result, the development and adoption of post-quantum cryptography will become imperative.

Post-quantum cryptography focuses on creating encryption algorithms that are resistant to quantum attacks. Researchers are exploring mathematical approaches and cryptographic primitives that can resist the computational power of quantum computers. In the future, organizations must transition to post-quantum encryption to secure their data and communications effectively.

As our society increasingly relies on interconnected cyber-physical systems (CPS) in sectors like energy, transportation, and healthcare, the protection of critical infrastructure will be a paramount concern. Cyberattacks targeting CPS can have devastating real-world consequences, including power outages, transportation disruptions, and compromised medical devices.

Securing critical infrastructure will require a holistic approach that combines robust cybersecurity measures, vulnerability assessments, and regulatory frameworks. Collaboration between government agencies, private sector organizations, and cybersecurity experts will be essential to safeguarding these vital systems from emerging threats.

The traditional perimeter-based security model is becoming less effective in a world where remote work and cloud computing are the norm. Zero-Trust Architecture assumes that no entity, whether inside or outside the organization, should be trusted by default, will gain prominence. Organizations will adopt a zero-trust approach to continuously verify user identities and devices before granting access to resources.

Secure Access Service Edge (SASE) will also play a crucial role in the future of cybersecurity. SASE combines network security and wide-area networking capabilities into a cloud-based service. This approach provides a flexible and scalable solution for securing remote and cloud-based environments, aligning with the evolving needs of organizations.

An increasing volume of threats and attack vectors marks the cybersecurity landscape. Organizations will embrace threat intelligence sharing and collaboration to combat these challenges effectively. Information sharing among industry peers, government agencies, and cybersecurity vendors will enable the rapid dissemination of threat indicators and attack patterns.

Collaborative cybersecurity efforts will extend to public-private partnerships, where government entities work closely with private sector organizations to enhance national cybersecurity resilience. By sharing threat intelligence, organizations can collectively strengthen their defenses and respond more effectively to cyber threats.

Data privacy and protection will remain at the forefront of cybersecurity concerns. Governments and regulatory bodies will continue introducing stringent data privacy laws and regulations. Organizations will be required to implement robust data protection measures, including encryption, data access controls, and transparency in data handling.

Cybersecurity professionals must navigate an increasingly complex landscape of data protection requirements, ensuring compliance with regulations like the European Union's GDRP, the California Consumer Privacy Act (CCPA), and other global data privacy laws. Privacy-enhancing technologies and practices will become essential components of cybersecurity strategies.

Cybersecurity is not solely a technical challenge; it also depends on the actions and behaviors of users. Phishing attacks, social engineering, and human errors continue to be significant security risks. In response, organizations will invest in enhanced user education and awareness programs.

User training will go beyond basic security practices and will focus on recognizing sophisticated threats and understanding the consequences of cybersecurity incidents. Organizations will promote a culture of cybersecurity awareness, making every employee a vital part of the defense against cyber threats.

As AI becomes more and more important in cybersecurity, questions of ethics and accountability will arise. AI algorithms can inadvertently perpetuate biases or make decisions that have unintended consequences. Cybersecurity professionals and organizations must address these ethical considerations when developing and deploying AI-powered security solutions.

Accountability mechanisms will also become critical. Ensuring that AI-driven cybersecurity systems are transparent, auditable, and accountable for their actions will maintain trust and prevent misuse of AI technologies.

In conclusion, the future of cybersecurity promises both challenges and opportunities. Cybersecurity professionals must remain adaptable and innovative as AI, quantum computing, and new technologies continue to shape the digital landscape. Collaboration, threat intelligence sharing, and a holistic approach to security will be vital in defending against emerging threats. Privacy, ethics, and user education will also ensure a secure and resilient digital future. As the cybersecurity landscape evolves, so too must our strategies and defenses to protect the ever-expanding digital world.

Preparing for evolving challenges

The world of cybersecurity is in a constant state of flux, driven by rapid technological advancements, the proliferation of digital devices, and the ingenuity of cybercriminals. As the digital landscape expands, so do the challenges and threats individuals, organizations, and nations face. To effectively navigate this dynamic environment, it is essential to prepare for the evolving challenges of cybersecurity. This section explores key strategies and considerations for staying ahead of cyber threats and building resilient defenses.

One of the foundational pillars of effective cybersecurity preparedness is continuous education and skill development. Cyber threats are ever-evolving, so cybersecurity professionals must stay updated with the latest trends, attack vectors, and defense strategies. This entails attending cybersecurity conferences, participating in training programs, and obtaining industry-recognized certifications.

The field of cybersecurity encompasses a wide range of roles and responsibilities, from ethical hacking and penetration testing to incident response and security analysis. Professionals in this field must cultivate a diverse skill set that includes technical proficiency, analytical thinking, problem-solving abilities, and effective communication. Staying current with programming languages, networking protocols, and security tools is crucial, as is understanding the psychology and motivations of cybercriminals.

IT departments are no longer the only ones accountable for cybersecurity. It has become an organizational-wide concern that demands a holistic approach to security. This means that cybersecurity considerations should be integrated into every aspect of an organization's operations, from product development and supply chain management to employee training and risk assessment.

Implementing a holistic cybersecurity strategy involves risk management, where organizations assess potential threats and vulnerabilities and develop mitigation plans. It also includes developing and enforcing security policies and procedures, ensuring that employees are educated about cybersecurity best practices, and regularly auditing and monitoring systems for potential breaches. Collaboration between different departments, including IT, legal, human resources, and management, is crucial to building a robust cybersecurity framework.

With today's sophisticated threats, traditional perimeter-based security solutions are no longer enough. A security approach known as "Zero Trust," which holds that no entity—internal or external to the company—should be trusted by default, is becoming more and more popular. Zero Trust entails verifying the identity of users and devices and continuously monitoring and controlling access to resources.

Additionally, the principle of least privilege should be applied, ensuring that users and systems are granted only the minimum level of access or permissions necessary to perform their tasks. This limits the potential impact of security breaches and reduces the attack surface available to malicious actors.

As cyber threats become more advanced, organizations are turning to artificial intelligence (AI) and machine learning (ML) to bolster their defenses. AI-powered cybersecurity systems can analyze huge amounts of data in real-time, detect anomalies, and identify potential threats with high accuracy. ML algorithms can adapt and learn from new data, making them valuable for threat detection and prevention.

However, it's essential to recognize that cybercriminals can also exploit AI and ML. AI-driven malware and automated attack tools can rapidly evolve and evade traditional security measures. Cybersecurity professionals must harness these technologies defensively while also staying vigilant for AI-driven threats.

Cyber threats are not confined by borders or industry sectors, making collaboration and threat intelligence sharing essential components of cybersecurity preparedness. Organizations should participate in industry-specific Information Sharing and Analysis Centers (ISACs) and collaborate with peers to share threat indicators, attack patterns, and best practices.

Public-private partnerships are also crucial for national and global cybersecurity resilience. Government agencies, private sector organizations, and cybersecurity experts must work together to strengthen defenses, respond to threats, and develop strategies for protecting critical infrastructure.

Despite best efforts to prevent cyberattacks, incidents can and do occur. An incident response plan that is well stated must be in place in order to reduce the impact of a breach. An incident response plan should set communication guidelines, specify roles and duties for both individuals and teams, and offer instructions for confining and reducing the incident.

Recovery planning is equally important. Organizations should regularly back up their data and systems, ensuring that critical information can be restored in the event of a ransomware attack or data breach. Testing and refining incident response and recovery plans through simulations and drills can help ensure their effectiveness when a real incident occurs.

Data privacy regulations are becoming increasingly stringent, with laws like General Data Protection Regulation (GDPR) of the European Union and the California Consumer Privacy Act (CCPA) setting new standards for data protection. Organizations must comply with these regulations, which often require robust data security measures, transparency in data handling, and prompt reporting of data breaches.

Failure to adhere with data privacy regulations can result in substantial fines and reputational damage. Therefore, organizations must establish strong data protection practices and regularly audit and assess their compliance to mitigate legal and financial risks.

Ethical considerations come to the forefront as AI and machine learning technologies become more integrated into cybersecurity operations. The use of AI in cybersecurity raises questions about transparency, bias, and accountability. Businesses and cybersecurity experts need to make sure AI-powered systems are unbiased and transparent in their decision-making.

Accountability mechanisms should be in place to trace the actions of AI systems and hold them responsible for their decisions. Ethical guidelines and standards for the utilization of AI in cybersecurity should be developed and adhered to, ensuring that these technologies are employed ethically and responsibly.

In conclusion, preparing for the evolving challenges of cybersecurity is a multifaceted endeavor that requires continuous education, a holistic approach to security, and the integration of advanced technologies. Cybersecurity professionals must adapt to the ever-changing threat landscape and work collaboratively to defend against cyberattacks. By embracing new strategies and staying vigilant, organizations can build resilience in the face of evolving cyber threats and safeguard their digital assets and data.

CONCLUSION

Recap of key points

Throughout this book, titled "Navigating Cybersecurity and Ethical Hacking: The Art of Ethical Hacking - Exploring Cybersecurity from Within," we have embarked on a comprehensive journey into the realm of cybersecurity, ethical hacking, and the evolving landscape of digital security. Here, we recap some of the key points and insights gathered from the various sections of this book.

We began by defining cybersecurity as the practice of protecting computer systems, networks, and data from theft, damage, or unauthorized access. It entails various strategies and technologies to safeguard digital assets in an increasingly interconnected world.

We explored cybersecurity's historical context and evolution, tracing its origins from the early days of computing to the modern era of advanced cyber threats. This historical perspective highlights the continuous need for innovative security measures to keep pace with evolving technologies.

We emphasized the critical importance of cybersecurity in the digital age, where virtually every aspect of our lives depends on interconnected technology. The consequences of security breaches can be serious, ranging from financial losses and privacy violations to threats to national security.

Our exploration into hacking elucidated that hacking is not inherently malicious. It can be categorized into ethical hacking (white hat), malicious hacking (black hat), and a gray area in between (gray hat). Ethical hackers are vital in identifying vulnerabilities and strengthening digital defenses.

Ethics in hacking is a foundational principle. Ethical hackers comply to a strict code of ethics, including obtaining proper authorization, protecting privacy, and reporting vulnerabilities responsibly. This ethical framework distinguishes them from malicious hackers.

We defined ethical hacking as the practice of intentionally probing computer systems, networks, or applications to identify security vulnerabilities before malicious hackers can exploit them. Ethical hackers use their skills for the greater good, helping organizations bolster their cybersecurity defenses.

In our exploration of ethical hacking, we contrasted it with malicious hacking, highlighting the crucial differences in intent and outcomes. While ethical hackers aim to enhance security, malicious hackers seek to exploit weaknesses for personal gain or harm.

We delved into the legal and ethical considerations surrounding ethical hacking. Proper authorization, consent, and adherence to legal frameworks are essential to conducting ethical hacking responsibly and within the bounds of the law.

Our exploration of common cyber threats encompassed viruses, malware, phishing attacks, and other tactics used by cybercriminals to compromise systems and steal data. Understanding these threats is critical for effective cybersecurity.

We discussed methods for identifying system vulnerabilities, including vulnerability scanning, penetration testing, and code reviews. Identifying weaknesses early is vital for preemptively addressing potential security risks.

Real-world examples of cyberattacks provided insights into the tangible consequences of security breaches. Notable incidents like the Equifax data breach and the

WannaCry ransomware attack illustrated the widespread impact of cyber threats.

We elucidated the steps in the hacking process, including reconnaissance, scanning, exploitation, maintaining access, and covering tracks. Understanding these phases helps organizations defend against potential attacks.

An exploration of the tools and techniques used by ethical hackers revealed the arsenal at their disposal. These resources are employed to assess and secure digital environments, from network scanners to password cracking tools.

We highlighted the value of hands-on exercises and demonstrations for ethical hackers. Practical experience, gained through activities like Capture The Flag (CTF) challenges and virtual labs, is essential for honing skills.

Our examination of penetration testing clarified its role in ethical hacking. Penetration testers simulate cyberattacks to identify vulnerabilities and weaknesses, providing organizations with actionable insights for improvement.

We differentiated between various types of penetration tests, including black-box, white-box, and grey-box testing. Each approach offers unique advantages and focuses on different aspects of security assessment.

We discussed the process of conducting a penetration test, emphasizing the importance of planning, testing, and reporting. Effective penetration testing requires a structured approach to uncover vulnerabilities.

We highlighted best practices for enhancing cybersecurity, including implementing security policies, securing endpoints, and staying vigilant against emerging threats. The key to staying protected when it comes to security is to be proactive.

Our exploration of security policies and procedures underscored their role in establishing a security-conscious organizational culture. Effective policies provide guidelines for safeguarding data and resources.

Finally, we emphasized the importance of security awareness training. Educating employees about cybersecurity best practices helps create a human firewall against threats like phishing and social engineering.

In conclusion, this book has provided a comprehensive overview of cybersecurity and ethical hacking, addressing fundamental concepts, strategies, and practical approaches to securing digital environments. The ever-evolving landscape of cybersecurity necessitates continuous learning and adaptation, underscoring the importance of staying informed and proactive in the face of emerging challenges. As technology advances, the principles and practices outlined in this book will remain essential for safeguarding the digital world.

The ongoing importance of ethical hacking

In an era defined by digital transformation, where technology permeates every facet of our lives, the importance of ethical hacking has never been more pronounced. Ethical hacking, often referred to as white-hat hacking or penetration testing, is the practice of probing computer networks, systems, as well as applications for security vulnerabilities to strengthen defenses. As the digital landscape expands and cyber threats grow increasingly sophisticated, ethical hacking remains a cornerstone in the ongoing battle to safeguard data, privacy, and critical infrastructure.

The first and foremost reason for the enduring significance of ethical hacking lies in the ever-evolving threat landscape. Malicious hackers, driven by financial gain, political motivations, or sheer mischief, constantly seek new ways to exploit vulnerabilities in digital systems. These threats manifest in various forms, from ransomware attacks that hold data hostage to phishing schemes that trick individuals into revealing sensitive information. Organizations and individuals must adopt a proactive approach to counter these threats effectively, identifying weaknesses before they are exploited. This proactive stance is precisely what ethical hacking embodies.

Armed with the knowledge and skills of their malicious counterparts, ethical hackers act as the vanguard in this digital battlefield. They employ the same tactics, techniques, and tools to uncover vulnerabilities and weaknesses in systems and networks. Doing so provides organizations with critical insights into their security posture, enabling them to remediate vulnerabilities and fortify their defenses. Ethical hackers serve as a vital bridge between the ever-evolving threat landscape and the defenders who strive to protect digital assets.

Moreover, ethical hacking serves as a litmus test for an organization's commitment to security and compliance. In an era where data breaches and cyberattacks can result in crippling financial losses and tarnished reputations, organizations are under increasing pressure to demonstrate robust cybersecurity practices. Ethical hacking, through processes such as penetration testing and vulnerability assessments, allows organizations to assess their readiness to withstand cyber threats and adhere to regulatory requirements. It enables them to identify areas for improvement, bolster security measures, and proactively address potential weaknesses before auditors or malicious actors do.

Another aspect of ethical hacking's ongoing importance is its role in staying ahead of emerging technologies and trends. As the digital landscape evolves, incorporating innovations such as the Internet of Things, cloud computing, and artificial intelligence, new attack surfaces and vulnerabilities emerge. Ethical hackers play a crucial role in staying abreast of these developments, devising strategies to assess and secure these technologies. They explore potential risks associated with IoT devices, cloud-based infrastructures, and AI-driven systems, ensuring that organizations can embrace innovation without compromising security.

Ethical hacking also contributes to building a culture of cybersecurity awareness. In organizations that prioritize security, the practice of ethical hacking fosters a mindset where security is not an afterthought but an integral part of operations. Employees become more vigilant against phishing attempts, social engineering attacks, and other common tactics malicious actors employ. Ethical hacking exercises, such as simulated phishing campaigns and security awareness training, empower individuals to recognize and report potential threats, thus augmenting the organization's overall security posture.

In conclusion, the ongoing importance of ethical hacking in our digital age cannot be overstated. It serves as a proactive defense against a relentless tide of cyber threats, providing organizations and individuals with the means to identify and remediate vulnerabilities before they are exploited. Ethical hacking contributes to regulatory compliance, adapts to emerging technologies, and cultivates a culture of cybersecurity awareness. In an ever-connected world, where the stakes for security are higher than ever, ethical hacking remains an indispensable tool in the arsenal of defenders committed to safeguarding our digital future.

Encouragement for readers to explore ethical hacking

Ethical hacking is a field of immense significance and opportunity in the rapidly evolving landscape of technology and cybersecurity. It represents a realm where curiosity meets responsibility, where the thrill of exploration combines with the duty to safeguard digital realms. As you've journeyed through this book, "Navigating Cybersecurity and Ethical Hacking: The Art of Ethical Hacking - Exploring Cybersecurity from Within," you've likely gained insights into the pivotal role that ethical hackers play in fortifying the digital world. Now, I want to encourage you to explore ethical hacking further and consider how it can become a part of your own journey.

One of the most compelling reasons to delve into ethical hacking is the sheer demand for skilled professionals in this field. The digital age has brought with it a proliferation of technology and an explosion of data. With this expansion comes an increased attack surface for cybercriminals who seek to exploit vulnerabilities for personal gain or malicious intent. Large and small organizations urgently require individuals with the expertise to identify and address these vulnerabilities. By pursuing a career in ethical hacking, you can become a guardian of the digital realm, helping organizations secure their data and protect their customers.

Furthermore, ethical hacking is a field that thrives on intellectual curiosity and problem-solving. It's a discipline that rewards those who relish challenges and possess a natural penchant for exploring the depths of technology. The thrill of uncovering hidden vulnerabilities, outsmarting malicious hackers, and devising creative solutions is a driving force for ethical hackers. Ethical hacking might be your ideal avenue to channel that energy if you've ever felt that innate curiosity when encountering a security puzzle.

Moreover, ethical hacking offers a unique opportunity to impact society positively. Beyond the monetary rewards, ethical hackers often find deep satisfaction in knowing that their work contributes to the greater good. By fortifying organizations' digital defenses, they help protect sensitive information, critical infrastructure, and even the privacy of individuals. This sense of purpose is a powerful motivator for those who wish to use their skills for a noble cause.

Embarking on a journey into ethical hacking also means embracing a continuous learning experience. Technology never stands still, and the field of cybersecurity evolves alongside it. This means that ethical hackers always adapt and acquire new knowledge and skills. Ethical hacking provides an exciting and ever-changing landscape if you thrive in an environment of lifelong learning and intellectual growth.

To start your journey into ethical hacking, you can begin by exploring educational resources and certifications. Courses and certifications like Certified Ethical Hacker (CEH), CompTIA Security+, as well as Certified Information Systems Security Professional (CISSP) offer structured paths for gaining knowledge and recognition in the field. Virtual labs and Capture The Flag (CTF) challenges provide hands-on opportunities to hone your skills.

Networking is also crucial in the world of ethical hacking. Engaging in online forums, attending conferences, visiting local or virtual meetups, and getting involved with the cybersecurity community can help you remain up to date on the newest trends and risks as well as interact with like-minded people. In this profession, cooperation and knowledge exchange are essential for success.

In conclusion, ethical hacking offers a thrilling and purposeful journey into the heart of cybersecurity. It combines intellectual curiosity, problem-solving, and a sense of duty to protect the digital realm. With a growing demand for skilled professionals, a commitment to lifelong learning, as well as a desire to create a positive impact, you can embark on a rewarding career in ethical hacking. As you continue your exploration, remember that the digital world needs individuals like you willing to explore its depths, uncover vulnerabilities, and be guardians of its security.

Thank you for buying and reading/ listening to our book. If you found this book useful/ helpful please take a few minutes and leave a review on the platform where you purchased our book. Your feedback matters greatly to us.